STORM WHIPPED COCONUT PALMS AT THE EDGE OF KAU DESERT

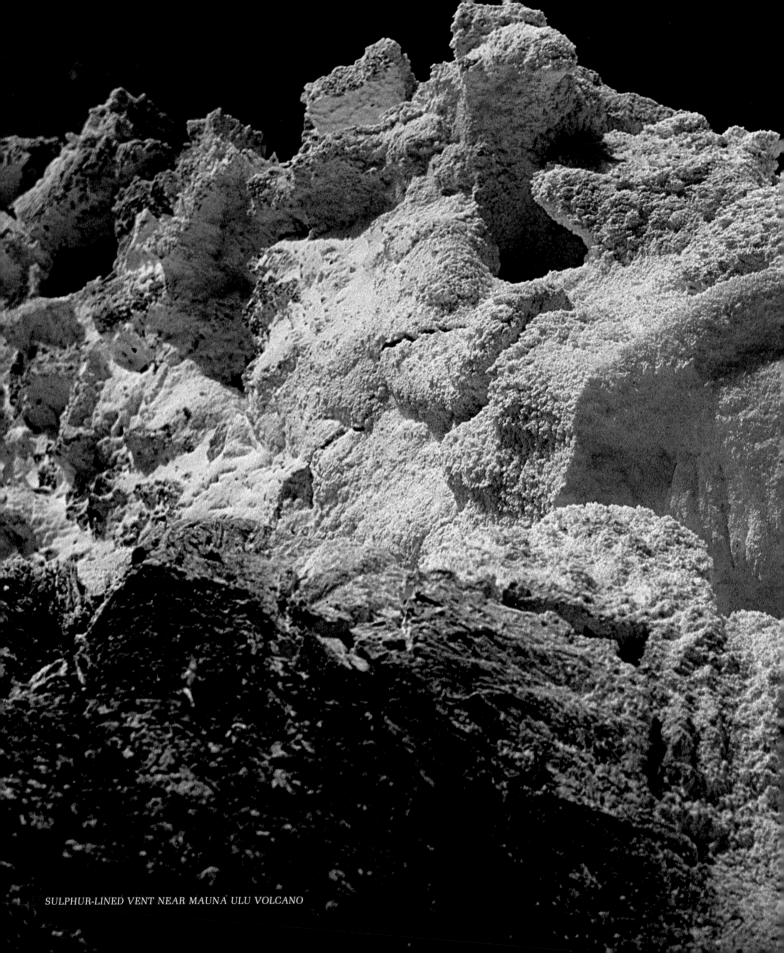

SULPHUR-LINED VENT NEAR MAUNA ULU VOLCANO

BLACK-FOOTED ALBATROSSES ON PEARL AND HERMES REEF

STARBURSTS OF THE ILIAU PLANT RIMMING WAIMEA CANYON

TIME
LIFE
BOOKS

HAWAII

THE WORLD'S WILD PLACES/TIME-LIFE BOOKS/AMSTERDAM

BY ROBERT WALLACE
AND THE EDITORS OF TIME-LIFE BOOKS

THE WORLD'S WILD PLACES

Editorial Staff for *Hawaii*:
EDITOR: Charles Osborne
Picture Editor: Iris Friedlander
Designer: Charles Mikolaycak
Staff Writers: Gerald Simons,
Simone D. Gossner, Anne Horan
Chief Researcher: Martha T. Goolrick
Researchers: Gail Cruikshank,
Terry Drucker, Beatrice Hsia, Carol Isenberg,
Michael Luftman, Don Nelson,
Ruth Silva
Design Assistant: Vincent Lewis

ISBN 7054 0160 X

TIME-LIFE is a trademark of Time Incorporated U.S.A.

Time-Life Books (Nederland) B.V.
Ottho Heldringstraat 5, 1066 AZ Amsterdam.

The Author: Robert Wallace is the author of several previous TIME-LIFE books: *The Rise of Russia* in the Great Ages of Man series; in the Library of Art, *The World of Van Gogh, The World of Rembrandt, The World of Leonardo* and *The World of Bernini*; and *The Grand Canyon* in The World's Wild Places series. He gathered the material for the present volume on visits to wild areas on the islands of Hawaii, Maui, Lanai, Molokai, Oahu and Kauai, and during a stay on uninhabited Pearl and Hermes Reef, a remote atoll in the Hawaiian archipelago.

The Cover: A branch of the Kalalau Stream courses through the valley of the same name, on the Island of Kauai. The eerie spires through which it winds were once part of the lava cliffs behind them, and have been separated and sculptured into their present shapes by millions of years of water erosion.

Contents

An Ancient Archipelago

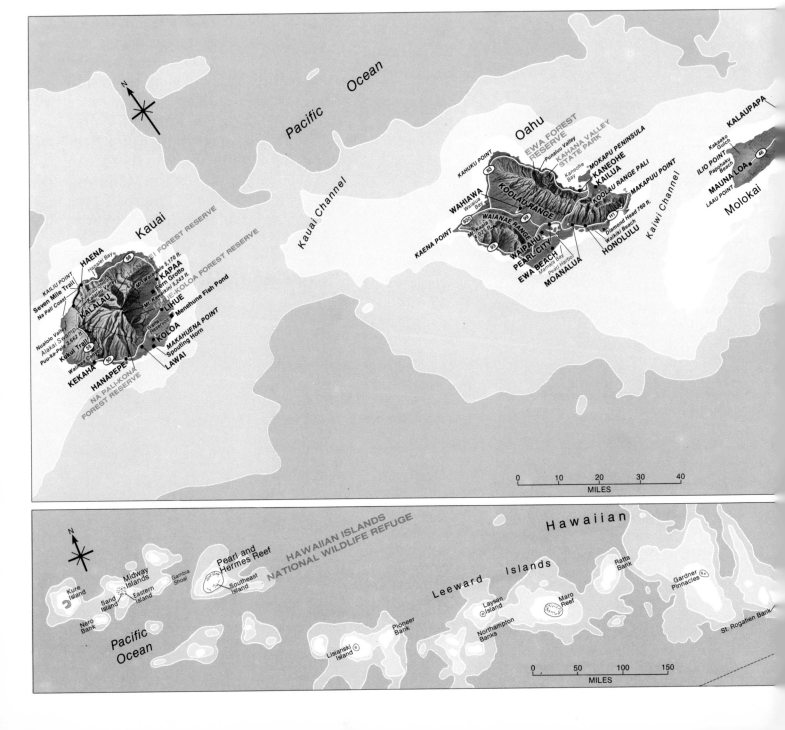

The long reach of the present-day Hawaiian archipelago, a chain of volcanic islands ranging in age from 700,000 years to 16 million years and stretching 1,600 miles across the mid-Pacific Ocean, is indicated by the green rectangle on the right and by the more detailed map at the bottom. Washed on all sides by the sea—its increasing depths shown by deepening shades of grey—the islands have a total area of 6,500 square miles. The oldest islands, such as Pearl and Hermes Reef, stand above sea level only because of coral built up on eroded volcanoes. (Still older islands, some of which rose 25 million years ago, are now entirely submerged.) The major islands at the eastern end of the chain (large relief map) emerged last. On one, Hawaii, there are active volcanoes. Green lines indicate rivers and streams. Red lines (on both maps) define the boundaries of parks and forest reserves. White lines represent major roads; black lines are trails. Black squares mark points of special interest.

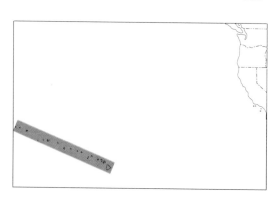

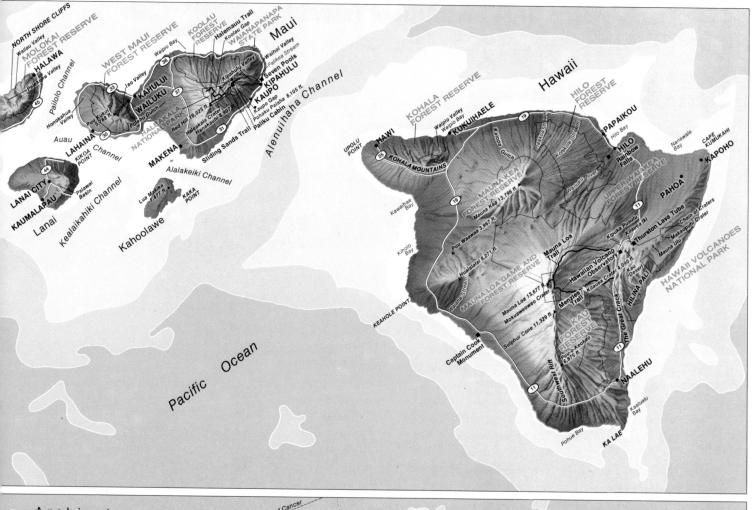

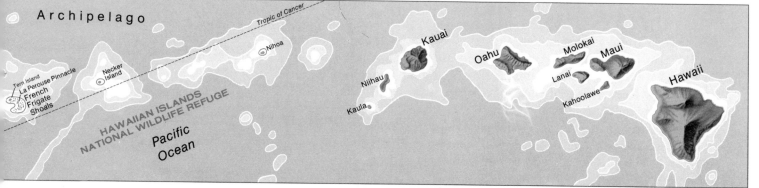

1/ A Handful of Jewels

*Midway across the North Pacific, space, time, and life
uniquely interlace a chain of islands named "Hawaiian"....
These small fragments of land appear offered to sky
by water and pressed to earth by stars.* CHARLES A. LINDBERGH

Even Americans find it difficult to believe that there is any wilderness
left in Hawaii. Waikiki has become Miami Beach West. Belief is hard
even for those who have taken a standard tour of several of the islands.
They wake each morning in what seems to be the same plastic hotel
room and at breakfast find the same small, mass-cultivated purple
orchid decorating their scrambled eggs. Yet the wilderness does exist;
and in fact some of the world's most naturally wild places exist
in the Hawaiian Islands. There are hidden valleys in Hawaii so remote, so overgrown with jungle and walled off by towering green-
black cliffs that few men have ever entered them. Year after year the
valleys are silent except for the spatter of rain on the canopy of
leaves, the splash of waterfalls and the call of birds. Faraway and mys-
terious, called by such Polynesian names as Waihoi and Kipahulu,
the valleys are in a sense among the experimental greenhouses of the
world. Many of the plants growing there, from the lowliest moss to
the loftiest trees, belong to unique species found nowhere else on
earth. Very likely a few of them have never even been glimpsed, let
alone named and classified by botanists.
  There is almost impenetrable wilderness in the wet mountains, where
the rainfall may exceed 50 feet a year; and on the slopes of the volcanoes, where floods of orange lava, cooling into metallic grey,
constantly change the face of the earth. And wilderness exists, too, in

the Leewards, the far outlying islands where the rarest of birds and seals are making a last stand against extinction.

The wilderness areas are small by continental standards, to be sure. No one expects the High Sierra in the middle of the Pacific. But the wild places of Hawaii are extremely valuable, a handful of jewels on the green velvet sea, and what they contain is to the mainlander wondrously strange: silverswords and quivering *lapalapa* trees, six-foot violets and birds with curved bills that draw nectar from curved flowers. These things are not only rare but delicate—out of this world and fragile as dreams. They are the plants and birds one imagines in the background of Shakespeare's *Tempest*. Touch them and they vanish. It is brutish to go blundering among them without knowing their nature, without knowing at least something of the singular, almost enchanted life of sea islands.

Many islands are created by erosion along the edges of continents. The gnawing of waves, currents and even of wind may cut a channel through a peninsula, isolating a bit of land that may be less than an acre in size or as large as Trinidad, nearly 2,000 square miles. A continental island of this sort is somewhat like Noah's Ark, launched with a living cargo that can reproduce itself. The flora and fauna of Trinidad are much the same as those in near-by regions of the parent continent, South America. But the case of Hawaii is far different.

There are eight major, or "high", Hawaiian islands—Niihau, Kauai, Oahu, Molokai, Lanai, Kahoolawe, Maui and Hawaii. The latter is much the largest and geologically the newest, and lends its name to the entire group. The eight are clustered fairly close together and contain 99.9 per cent of the land area of the state. However, there are more than 100 other visible islets, atolls, pinnacles and shoals in the Hawaiian archipelago, which is 1,600 miles long and stretches far out into the north central Pacific to include Midway and Kure, which are mere atolls. Most of these remote dots of land—among them French Frigate Shoals, St. Rogatien Bank, Laysan Island, Lisianski Island and Pearl and Hermes Reef—are administered as part of the city and county of Honolulu, which, as a result, is 540,000 square miles in area and includes a good many more whales in its population than other cities.

Despite the length of the archipelago, it occupies only a tiny fraction of the vast Pacific and its situation is isolated and lonely indeed. From the eastern end of the Hawaiian chain it is 2,000 miles to San Francisco; from the centre, 2,400 miles north to the Aleutians; from the western end, 2,400 miles to Japan. To the south the first really major landfall is Antarctica, 7,000 miles away. Thus it is apparent that the Hawaiian Islands are not continental in origin. They were never attached to any mainland. How then did they get out there?

The islands are all volcanic. They arose from the bottom of the sea. To a layman the idea is stunning. Consider it. The Pacific is very deep in the neighbourhood of the archipelago, about 18,000 feet; and although it has been shallower in earlier times, the volcanic eruptions must still have occurred at great depth. They are among the most eerie events that have ever taken place in the natural world. Three miles deep in the ocean it is totally dark, extremely cold, and the pressure of the water is about three and a half tons to the square inch. In this crushing blackness a fissure opens and incandescent molten rock gushes out of it. The clash of light and dark, heat and cold, pressure and counterpressure is almost too much for the mind to grasp. No man has seen such a thing and only deduction can tell him what it is like. Although it might seem certain that there would be a prodigious explosion, there is none at all. The weight of the water contains it. Instead the lava, rapidly cooling, spills out quietly on the ocean floor. Not even a bubble of gas arises. On the face of the sea there is no sign of the fantastic event below.

As eruptions continue, layer upon layer of lava spreads across the sea bottom. During a few million years a mountain takes shape and slowly the pressure on its summit diminishes as it nears the surface. At last clouds of steam burst out of the ocean; fragments of rock are thrown up and fall back into the boiling water; and the volcano thrusts clear of the surface and keeps on growing. In this manner the Hawaiian chain has been formed. On the island of Hawaii two volcanoes, Kilauea and Mauna Loa, are still erupting. The latter has reached a height of 13,680 feet above sea level while near-by Mauna Kea, which is probably though not certainly extinct, stands at 13,796.

When the islands emerged from the Pacific they were quite the opposite of Noah's Ark. They were sterile, as antiseptic as it is possible for anything in nature to be. The temperature of molten lava can be as high as 2,200°F., intolerable to any form of life. Even the marine organisms in the ocean near by must have been killed when the water boiled. Yet in time the steaming lava cooled and became populated with a great variety of living things. The population had some broad gaps—the only mammals that reached the islands unaided by man were bats and seals. Many plant species made the journey but, oddly, no conifers. Land snails arrived in large numbers; amphibians and reptiles never did, except for the green sea turtle. Still, it is impressive that the islands should have been reached and colonized by so many species, all of which were obliged to cross many hundreds of miles of open sea.

There are three ways—setting aside the agency of man—in which the plants and creatures may have travelled: by drifting in the water, sailing on the wind, or by attaching themselves to other organisms. The spores of ferns, lichens and fungi are so small and light that they can be carried enormous distances in the air. The seeds of a few flowering plants, particularly orchids, are so tiny that they too can be airborne for hundreds of miles. Heavier seeds may drift in ocean currents. Others, indigestible but contained in edible fruits, may be eaten by shore birds and waterfowl and transported overseas. Experiments by biologists in recent years have shown that certain birds may retain seeds in their bodies for hundreds of hours. Still other seeds, either burrlike or covered with sticky coatings, may cling to birds' feet and feathers. Among sea birds the wide-ranging albatrosses, petrels, shearwaters, terns and boobies would have had little difficulty in reaching Hawaii. Several species of shore birds, among them the Pacific golden plover and the ruddy turnstone, migrate to Hawaii from the mainland each year; some of them remain for the winter and others pass on to more tropical islands. Small land birds, however, probably made the journey while caught in storms, and bats doubtless arrived in the same way.

Dr. Elwood C. Zimmerman, author of the classic *Insects of Hawaii*, wrote of a means of travel known as rafting. "Large rafts or masses of debris making up 'floating islands' are commonly washed out to sea. . . . A survey of these rafts probably would reveal that numerous plants and animals were riding them. . . . It is possible that some of them, on rare occasions, could travel more or less intact for many hundreds of miles and deposit at least part of their living cargoes on foreign shores. I have seen large trees washed from stream sides during a storm in Tahiti and have seen them floating out to sea with their large branches riding high out of the water. . . . Some of the branches may be held 20 or more feet above the waves. . . . It is conceivable that over a period of several millions of years a few such floating trees have been beached in Hawaii and that from them there escaped ancestors of some of our insects, terrestrial molluscs and plants."

The odds against any particular species reaching Hawaii and becoming established were immense. But so is geological time. The botanist F. Raymond Fosberg estimates that more than 1,700 species of flowering plants now found in Hawaii had only about 275 ancestors, and

Towering above a stand of withered ohia trees and coco palms, fiery lava and billowing steam rise from the main vent of the Kapoho cinder cone, which is situated in a rift zone of Kilauea Volcano. The picture was taken during the volcano's longest eruption of this century: it began in early October 1959 and continued in three stages until mid-February 1960.

that in the 25 million years since the first of the islands emerged from the sea there need only have been one successful colonization of seed plants every 20,000 years. Thus it is not surprising that Hawaii has a substantial, varied plant and animal population and that its progenitors have journeyed there from North, Central and South America, Australia, Asia, other Pacific Islands and perhaps even Africa.

Upon reaching the islands the ancestral plants, insects and birds encountered circumstances quite different from those in which they had earlier evolved. In general these circumstances were easier, more free, less competitive. A good many plants, for example, have developed strong defences against being eaten by sheep, goats, cattle and wild herbivores. The plants have sharp thorns, a rank smell, a bad taste. They may also be poisonous. But in ancient times there were no herbivores in Hawaii and the plants' defences were unnecessary. Therefore in the inexorable logic of nature the defences were bred out; they vanished. Now there are very few native plants with thorns, only one or two that are poisonous and none that are particularly foul-smelling. Another characteristic of Hawaiian plants, even those that are not consumed by cattle and goats, is their lack of aggressiveness. Their mainland ancestors were obliged to fight for moisture and places in the sun, and no doubt the Hawaiian immigrants still possessed the same toughness when they arrived in the islands. But there they found ample space, moisture and sun and their competitiveness slowly diminished.

While the plants (and insects and birds) were becoming, in an anthropomorphic sense, meek, they were also changing into new species. As they spread out into the many small environments or microclimates of the islands, wet and dry, high and low, they underwent a process called adaptive radiation. Different foods, temperatures, humidities and other factors caused them to change in habit and appearance, often so drastically that they no longer bore much resemblance to their common ancestors. The range of local environments in Hawaii is remarkable. Consider rainfall. The summit of Mount Waialeale on the island of Kauai is the rainiest place in the world. The constant trade winds blowing from the northeast are heavily burdened with moisture. When they reach the mountain they are forced upwards. This rising causes the air to cool, condensing the moisture, which then falls as incredible torrents of rain. As much as 50 feet of rain a year drops on Waialeale and into the near-by Alakai Swamp, a depression on a slope of the ancient volcano. The plants that live there are, to say the least, unusual. Yet within a very few miles, in the "rain shadow" of the mountain where almost all the moisture has been removed from the air, other plants have evolved in near-desert conditions. While the islands' temperature range in the valleys is mild, there are extremes (at least for subtropical islands) of heat and cold. On any night of the year the temperature may fall below freezing on the nearly 14,000-foot peaks of Mauna Loa and Mauna Kea on Hawaii; a dust of snow often covers their tops in winter. Not far away the climate is always balmy. Throughout the islands, because of local differences in soil, moisture, exposure, altitude, temperature and wind, there are isolated colonies of plants whose range may be only a couple of hundred yards.

Hand in hand with adaptive radiation went two other factors that have made the Hawaiian plant and animal population unique on earth. Most of the plants and birds are the descendants of a few individuals —in the case of plants, perhaps only one—and show the results of prolonged inbreeding. In continental areas many members of the same species from broad geographical regions are constantly crossbreeding and thus the species as a whole tends to remain the same. Variants and eccentrics do appear, but crossbreeding suppresses or absorbs them. However, in a small island community where little or no fresh genetic material can be added in the breeding process, individual eccentricities may be emphasized and new species are created fairly quickly.

The second factor that has led to rapid speciation—the biologists' word for the process by which new species are formed—lies in the volcanic origin of Hawaii. Lava is not uniform in hardness; some of it is easily eroded, some very durable. However, a glance at the awesome cliffs pictured on pages 165 and 168, for example, makes plain that the forces of rain, wind and waves have deeply carved the face of the islands. In some areas sharp ridges and pinnacles, separated by sheer-walled valleys, have become in effect islands upon islands. It is difficult or impossible for certain plants and creatures—land snails, for example —to move from one ridge to another and thus they have become doubly marooned and even more likely to develop into new species.

Today there are about 1,660 species of flowering plants in Hawaii that are classified as endemic—that is, they are found nowhere else on earth. Another 100 species are indigenous, growing naturally in Hawaii but also found elsewhere. Beyond these there are scores of exotic plants, introduced purposely or accidentally by man, that come from all parts of the globe. Among birds there are perhaps 45 endemic species still surviving; the exact number is unknown because a few rare individuals may—or may not—still be found in remote valleys and mountain jungles. One might suppose that the discovery in Hawaii of 1,660 plants and 45 birds new to science would be a source of joy unconfined, certainly among botanists and ornithologists. And to be sure, it has been. But the sense of joy has long since been replaced by anxiety and gloom because of the destruction of these unique species by man and by the alien plants, animals and diseases that man has imported. Within the past 200 years at least 25 endemic birds have become extinct in Hawaii. The number of plants that have been exterminated by men, sheep and goats cannot be determined with great accuracy (some plants may well have disappeared before botanists ever saw them), but it is surely large. As the botanist Sherwin Carlquist puts it, "there have been more animal and plant species extinguished in the Hawaiian Islands than in the entirety of North America".

One major reason for the mass extinction has already been suggest-

When Captain James Cook explored the Hawaiian Islands in early 1779, the people believed him to be one of their gods and feted him royally. But a fracas that ensued from the theft of a dory from his flagship cost the celebrated Englishman his life. In this 19th Century engraving of the incident, Cook is the figure with outstretched arm, about to be stabbed in the back.

ed: the peculiar passivity, the Eden innocence of island species. Its complement is the peculiar virulence of introduced species. The idea may be extended without too great distortion into the world of men. In 1778, when Captain James Cook of the British Navy discovered the islands, he was well aware of certain dangers. ("Discovered" is an unpopular word among Hawaiians. Cook was indeed the first European to find the islands, but Polynesian navigators of great skill and daring discovered them about 1,000 years before he did.) Cook's fear was that his crew would spread venereal disease among the natives. In contrast to the stereotype of callous skippers roistering across the Pacific leaving syphilis on every atoll and not caring a damn, Cook was an intelligent, decent soul. Unfortunately his efforts at quarantine were foredoomed—after glancing at his lusty sailors and the half-naked maidens swarming around them, he gloomily confided to his journal that "No women I ever met with were less reserved. Indeed, it appeared to me that they visited us with no other view than to make a surrender of their persons." Still, Cook tried. He ordered the crews of his small boat not to go ashore and "all female visitors to be excluded from the ships. Many of them had come off in the canoes. . . . They would as readily have favoured us with their company on board as the men; but I wished to prevent all connection which might, too probably, convey an irreparable injury to themselves, and through their means to the whole nation. . . . Whether these regulations, dictated by humanity, had the desired effect or not, only time can discover."

Within two weeks of Cook's arrival the infection had been spread. A party of men who had been sent ashore to trade was held on the beach by heavy surf for two days and nights and somehow neglected to remember the captain's orders. Although Cook was chiefly concerned with one disease there were others to which the natives were disastrously susceptible. Epidemics of smallpox, measles and influenza brought in by subsequent colonists reduced the population from about 300,000 at the time of the discovery to 50,000 a century later. Today there may be fewer than 8,000 pure-blooded Hawaiians left, largely because of the ravages of disease and in part because of interbreeding with the many foreign races that have come to live in the islands.

The introduction of exotic species among plants has had an effect comparable to the introduction of germs and viruses among men. The lantana, which on the American mainland is a modest, maidenly flower sometimes used in borders of home gardens, becomes tigerish in the nourishing climate of Hawaii. It grows 8 or 10 feet tall, develops thorns

The pandanus or hala tree, a form of
screw pine, carpets the Puhaluu Valley
on Oahu. The plant, introduced to the
Hawaiian Islands by the colonizing
Polynesians about 1,000 years ago, now
thrives along the islands' shorelines.

and goes rampaging across the countryside. Fireweeds, guavas and blackberries have spread explosively in many areas, overwhelming native species that could not compete with them. On the island of Oahu, by far the most developed of the group, about 85 per cent of all the native vegetation has been wiped out and replaced by plants brought in by man. Today the importation of foreign species is subject to strict legal control but the laws are largely too late.

Cattle, pigs and goats have been ruinously destructive in Hawaii almost from the days of their introduction. Polynesian colonizers brought the pigs, and apparently also brought rats as stowaways in their great seagoing canoes. Captain Cook fetched goats to the islands in 1778; his fellow British explorer, George Vancouver, introduced cattle and sheep in 1793. Each of the animals is a menace in its own fashion. Wild pigs are particularly troublesome because of their habit of rooting up large areas of the forest floor. The freshly turned earth affords a lodgment for foreign plants that might not otherwise be able to take hold and multiply. Goats, which both graze and browse, eat the native grasses down to the roots and destroy small trees and shrubs by devouring their twigs and tearing off their bark. Cattle, pastured in the uplands that once were forest, eat and trample rare plants well-nigh at will. Botanist Carlquist in *Hawaii: A Natural History* writes of *Delissea undulata*, a fantastic relative of the common lobelias of many flower gardens. The plant has white-and-green flowers and purple-black fruit, clustered at the top of a bare, 20-foot fish-pole stem that enables it to reach up towards the light in dense forests. "*Delissea undulata* was very nearly extinct when I saw it in 1966, when 23 plants were counted in the one cinder cone where it was known to have survived," Carlquist reported. "At that time one could see plants only recently demolished by cattle or pigs. Most of the remaining plants were fenced off in 1967 and this curious plant may have been saved."

Goats and pigs run wild in the islands; cattle once did, but now are confined to ranches, some of which are surprisingly large; the Parker Ranch on the island of Hawaii has 250,000 acres. In the 19th Century cowboys on the Parker Ranch, to preserve the purity of their breed of cattle, killed all the wild bulls and cows they could find. Many were captured in pitfalls on the slopes of Mauna Kea, and in one of these pitfalls —probably not by accident—an eminent botanist met his death. The man was David Douglas, who had botanized along the west coast of North America and given his name to a number of plants, including the Douglas fir. When Douglas climbed Mauna Kea in search of new specimens he was accompanied by an ex-convict who, it seems likely, shoved him into a pit where a bull gored and trampled him to death.

The destructiveness of domestic animals gone wild, particularly goats and pigs, seems unlikely to be curbed until they are wiped out. Hawaiians hunt and eat them but do not kill enough to make much of a dent in the population—the breeding potential of wild goats is such that 100 of them in 15 years can increase to about 20,000. Recently on the island of Hawaii alone as many as 18,000 of the animals have been wandering ravenously across the land. Although extermination is preferable, another means of dealing with goats is to fence them out of certain areas. In 1972 in Hawaii Volcanoes National Park the rangers, after great labour, fenced a 2,500-acre area to keep goats out, at a cost of £1,600 for each mile of its three-and-a-half-mile-long fence. It is not easy to drill postholes in lava. The close-cropped vegetation in this large enclosure may revive and flourish, as it already has in an experimental one-acre enclosure fenced a couple of years ago. Indeed, a very startling and heartening event took place in this enclosure not long after it was completed. The grass returned, its leaves providing shade and its roots holding moisture, and then among the tufts of grass there appeared a plant the rangers had never seen before. It proved to be a pea-like vine, hitherto unclassified and unknown, a new species. Apparently its seed had lain dormant in the ground for half a century or more awaiting the right opportunity to sprout.

There are other encouraging gleams and glimmers in the dark Hawaiian scene. Birds thought to be extinct have been found in Kipahulu Valley on Maui and in the Alakai Swamp on Kauai. A new tree belonging to a rare genus has been found deep in Kauai's Waimea Canyon. The creatures that inhabit the remote outlying islands are holding their own. As to the choice of wilderness areas that are described and pictured in this book, it may be well to repeat what was earlier said of them: there are many such areas, small and jewel-like. To include the Na Pali coast of Kauai is not intentionally to slight the north coast of Molokai; a discussion of Kipahulu on Maui is not meant to denigrate Moanalua on Oahu or any of a score of other wild places beloved by Hawaiians. It is only a question of choosing among riches.

An Island Chain Forged by Fire

The ancient Hawaiians drew comfort from a legend that the same great lava flows that occasionally devastated their fields also built up their islands. About a century ago scientific fact began to catch up with the myth. The Hawaiian archipelago, geologists realized, was an island chain stretching some 2,100 miles roughly northwest and encompassing the Leeward Islands. It was also noted that the island of Hawaii, the southernmost point in the archipelago, was geologically young—relatively unaltered by erosion and very active volcanically—while the other end of the chain consisted of extinct remnants of much older volcanoes.

These observations led scientists to conclude that all the islands in the chain were peaks in a colossal submarine ridge built up by lava flows from an enormous crack in the ocean floor. To account for the differences in the islands' ages, they suggested that the land-building eruptions had begun at the northwestern end of the crack and proceeded slowly southeastwards over millions of years. Confirmation that the Hawaiian Islands were formed more recently than the Leeward Islands came in the 1960s, with the development of radioactive dating methods.

But a radical new theory has been advanced to explain the formation of the island chain. According to this concept, the part of the earth's crust that underlies the chain consists of a continent-sized plate that for ages has been slipping northwestwards at a rate of about four inches a year. Beneath this vast plate, and centred at a point slightly to the north of the island of Hawaii, is a stationary "hot spot" of magma, about 175 miles in diameter, that spews up tremendous volumes of lava—perhaps through weak points in the plate—as the plate slides across the hot spot. The lava forms new islands, but as the plate carries them beyond the hot spot, they are no longer subject to lava flows, and ultimately succumb to the forces of erosion.

Graphic evidence of this theory appears in the photographs on the following pages. Most of the Hawaiian Islands have already slid northwestwards past the hot spot; their volcanoes are extinct and in time they will be worn down to fragments resembling the Leeward Islands of today. Yet even now, under 15,000 feet of water south of the island of Hawaii, earth tremors and incipient volcanoes suggest that new islands will eventually be formed.

Shooting as high as 1,900 feet, a fiery fountain of lava and gases erupts from a crater on Kilauea Volcano on the island of Hawaii. In time, when the lava flow solidifies and cools, it will create new areas of land; meanwhile the temperatures within this lava fountain range from approximately 2,000°F. at the yellowish-red core to 1,200°F. at the darker red fringes.

Kilauea: the Youngest, Liveliest Land-Builder

On the southeastern shore of Hawaii —youngest and southernmost island in the archipelago—is its youngest and most active volcano: Kilauea. Local seismographs have registered literally millions of earth tremors signalling lava movements within the mountain. The focal point of these churnings is the Halemaumau fire pit, a lake of molten lava in the four-square-mile caldera on top of the mountain. When the lake is full, the lava in it circulates constantly; the surface cools and forms a rocky crust that convectional currents in the lake continually pull under to melt again. Occasionally, prodigious up-wellings cause the lake to overflow. In a series of eruptions between 1967 and 1968 Halemaumau gushed incandescent lava (*right*) at the rate of 1.5 million cubic yards per hour.

For all these pyrotechnics at the top, the lava eruptions chiefly responsible for the recent building up of Kilauea and the land around it come from two long rift zones on the volcano's broad flanks. The numerous vents along these rifts sometimes eject great boulders and tons of cinders, but for the most part the lava that pours forth is so thin and fluid that great molten rivers have flowed downhill at 35 miles per hour and travelled 12 miles before they congealed. When such streams hit the sea below Kilauea to extend the land-building process, the result is often an inferno of smoke, steam and fire (*overleaf*).

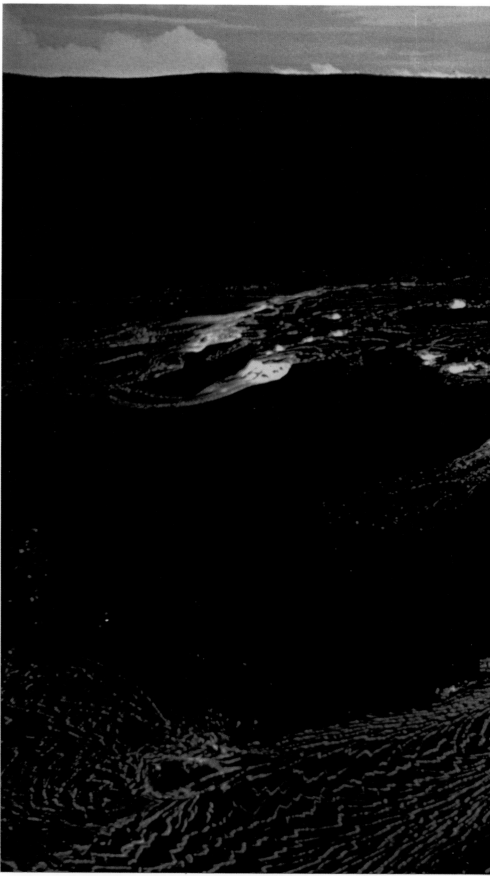

Halemaumau, a lava lake inside Kilauea's deep caldera, overflows in 1968, engulfing

about 1.6 square miles of the caldera floor. The rising lake built its own retaining walls as molten lava cooled and hardened around it.

Roaring down from Kilauea, steaming streams of pahoehoe lava, a thin, ropy variety, pour over a sea cliff in 1971. This eruption lasted three months and created 100 acres of new land.

Flowing from Kilauea's east rift zone in 1955, aa lava, chunky and slower-moving than pahoehoe lava, explodes on contact with the sea, forming black sand particles for Hawaiian beaches.

The gently sloping profile of western Maui's volcano typifies the classic shield shape of all Hawaiian volcanoes before erosion transforms

them. Lava that is unusually free-flowing, hence far-ranging, accounts for the shape.

A Tranquil, Ageing Volcano

The island of Maui, 30 miles northwest of Hawaii, is perhaps a million years older, and two volcanoes on its eastern and western ends have reached later stages in their geological life cycle. Land-building lava flows on western Maui's volcano (*left*) ceased entirely about 10,000 years ago, leaving the forces of erosion unopposed. Though they have not yet altered the exterior shield profile of the volcano, they have reduced its interior to a gutted shell. The caldera at the summit, a great cavity left when the mountain's empty magma chambers collapsed under the weight of ejected lava, has been worn down some 1,200 feet; at the same time the height of the summit rimming the crater has been lowered —almost a half-mile—from its former 7,000 feet to 5,700 feet.

Erosion on an even grander scale has eaten away at eastern Maui's huge volcano, 10,000-foot-high Haleakala. Its main crater, in fact, was created not by volcanic activity, as is usually the case, but by the erosive power of water. Sometime in the remote past, protracted torrential rainfall wore away as much as 3,000 feet of the volcano's summit and gouged canyons thousands of feet deeper into the heart of the mountain. When volcanic activity later resumed, and before it eventually stopped around the end of the 18th Century, new lava flows slowly filled the canyons and built up the plateaulike floor of today's crater (*overleaf*).

Eastern Maui's Haleakala Crater, hollowed out by long erosion and later overlaid with lava flows, is now an immense oval bowl seven miles long, two miles wide and half a mile deep. The photograph at left, taken from the crater's rim, reveals rain-carved inner walls with a much gentler slope than the steep sides of a crater formed by volcanic action. The jagged pinnacle in the foreground, contrasting vividly with the smooth cinder cone beyond, is a so-called dyke—a finger of lava that filled a crack in the crater wall, hardened, and was exposed when the softer material around it eroded. A view of the crater from the air (above) reveals a line of cinder cones that crosses the crater along a rift zone. From the vents below these cones came the lava flows that raised the crater floor to the level seen here. The reddish tint of the entire rockscape results from iron oxides in the lava.

Dense plant life and silvery waterfalls on Mount Waialeale, seen from a plane, give evidence of rain water's impact on an extinct volcano.

The Changes Wrought by Rainfall

The moaning of the trade winds is a kind of dirge for Kauai, the oldest major island in the Hawaiian archipelago. Buffeting Kauai from the northeast, the moisture-laden winds dump more and more rain as they blow inland, up the long broad slope of Mount Waialeale, the extinct volcano that long ago built up the island. The mountain's upper slope, a nearly vertical wall (*left*), is the wettest place on earth, with an average annual rainfall of 450 inches.

This incredible deluge nurtures such lush vegetation that Hawaiians call Kauai the "Garden Island". But as the rain drains downhill in streams laden with abrasive debris, it hastens the island's destruction. Waialeale's vast crater—the largest in the islands, 10 to 12 miles across —has already become a broken-down, overgrown Eden. On Kauai's north coast, erosion has carved out a colossal valley amphitheatre and slashed its walls with many secondary valleys (*right*). Succumbing to this relentless attack, the Kauai of the future will much resemble the present-day remnants of islands farther to the north (*overleaf*).

Water-carved buttresses form a sombre line along the west ridge of Kalalau Valley.

A fragment of volcanic rock, 910 feet high at its peak, is all that remains of Nihoa Island.

The Final Ravages of Time and Water

Once-active volcanoes, the 12 Leeward Islands, which extend the Hawaiian archipelago more than 1,200 miles to the northwest of the main islands, are the oldest links in the island chain and the most battered by time and erosion. Each successive Leeward island is older than the one to its southeast and hence displays greater ravages by wind, rain and sea. On Nihoa, the second youngest of the Leewards and some 2.3 million years older than the island of Hawaii, land-building lava flows that countered the forces of erosion ceased so long ago that the island, once 20 miles across, has shrunk to a rock one quarter of a square mile in area (*left*). Ages of rainfall and wave action have even more thoroughly worn down Kure (*right*), the oldest and outermost of the Leewards, at one point lowering it to sea level. But the shell of its volcano provided a foundation on which tiny sea creatures slowly built up a spacious, gleaming white coral atoll.

The low-lying atoll of Kure, oldest point in the island chain, outlines the site where a great volcano once towered above the sea.

2/ The Fire Goddess

*The fire-rivers, already rushing to the sea, were narrowed
and driven downward so rapidly that they leaped out from
the land, becoming immediately the prey of the remorseless
ocean.* WILLIAM D. WESTERVELT/ *HAWAIIAN LEGENDS OF VOLCANOES*

Kaha-wali was a chief who enjoyed sledging. Lacking snow, except on
the relatively inaccessible summits of Mauna Loa and Mauna Kea, the
Hawaiians slid down steep slopes covered with dry grass. Their one-
man sledges were long and very narrow, with polished hardwood runners
only a few inches apart, and they went so fast they scorched the grass.
One day when Kaha-wali was sporting on Kilauea he was approached
by an ugly old woman who asked to borrow his sledge. Foolishly, he re-
fused. Kaha-wali should have known who the woman was: the goddess
of volcanoes, Pele—in Hawaiian pronunciation, *pay-lay*. Sometimes
Pele goes among mortals as a crone, asking for help or a loan of some
sort. Sometimes she appears as a beautiful young woman, demanding
that a man sleep with her. When she is turned down she gets angry.

As soon as Kaha-wali spurned her request Pele's eyes turned to glowing coals and her hair to a banner of flame. She stamped on the ground,
opening a fissure from which lava burst forth. Kaha-wali flopped on his
sledge and rode for his life downhill while floods of molten rock pursued
him, Pele riding on the foremost billow. When his sledge ran out of mo-
mentum he scrambled to his feet and raced towards the ocean. On the
way he passed his mother and yelled, "Aloha ino oe eia ihonei paha oe
e make ai, ke ai manei Pele!" (May you receive mercy, because your
death is probably close at hand. Pele comes devouring.) Then he passed
his wife, who suggested that he remain with her so that they might die

together. Kaha-wali thanked her but kept on running. Then he passed his pet pig, whose name was Aloi-puaa. Kaha-wali paused to greet the pig by rubbing noses but he did not linger. Finally he came to the beach, one jump ahead of the lava, leaped into a canoe and saved himself while Pele threw hot rocks at him.

Hawaiians were afraid that ignorant and inexperienced visitors might not believe this story without corroborative evidence, so they immediately began to collect a mass of it, which they can produce when asked. One of the first men who asked was the Reverend William Ellis, an English missionary, who toured the site in 1823. The Hawaiians showed him the very hill where the incident took place. Ellis described it as "a black frowning crater about one hundred feet high, with a deep gap in the rim on the eastern side (towards the sea) from which the course of a current of lava could be distinctly traced". What is more, Kaha-wali's mother, his wife and his pig can all be seen turned to stone in the lava flow, and if a man goes snorkeling off the beach he can see strewn on the bottom the volcanic rocks Pele threw.

There are many stories of Pele in the written and unwritten literature of Hawaii and most of them have curious inverted nubs of truth in them, hyacinths planted upside down. The Hawaiians were keen and articulate observers of the natural world and their myths are like those of ancient Greece, full of apt explanations of events that scientists do not fully understand even now. Lava *does* suddenly burst out of the ground and rush downhill at surprising speed; it does harden around the shapes of living things; volcanic projectiles do splash into the sea. Hawaiians have on occasion been obliged to flee to safety in canoes.

The story of Kaha-wali accounts for some particular bits of local scenery; the tales of Pele herself explain the past and present volcanic activity in all the islands. Why is it that the volcanoes in the northwest are cold and dead, those in the central islands seemingly still warm, and those in the southeast vigorously erupting? The answer is Pele. At some ancient time she came to Hawaii to build a home, or rather to dig one. She likes to live in deep pits lined with fire. At first she dug on the island of Kauai, where she threw up a great mound of cinders called Puu-o-Pele, the hill of Pele, but sea water seeped into the pit and put out her flames. Then she moved southeast to Oahu and made several more pits and mounds with the same result. The last of these was Diamond Head, which is so close to the sea that it must have become uninhabitable for her very quickly. Pele moved on to Molokai, Lanai and then to Maui, where she was able to live until fairly recently in the immense crater of Haleakala. When her fire was extinguished there she went at last to the southeasternmost island, Hawaii, where she dug *two* homes that she still inhabits. The higher of the two, on the summit of 13,680-foot Mauna Loa, she has temporarily abandoned for the more salubrious climate of lower altitudes. She has not been seen there in 20 years, although she will surely be back. Her lower, favourite residence is in the fire pit of 4,090-foot Kilauea, from which smoke and fumes rise night and day. The volcano, one of the most active on earth, has been in almost continuous eruption in recent years, mainly from vents on its flanks where Pele can be seen swimming in the orange-hot lava.

Hawaiians still have a proverb that says "Watch out for old ladies; one of them may be Pele", and the goddess remains a real and terrifying presence to more than a few people who live within sight of Mauna Loa and Kilauea. In recent years offerings of roast meat and papayas have been tossed into lava flows to placate her. To the majority of Hawaiians, however, Pele has become only an outworn memory. The decline of her influence was hastened by an act of magnificent courage on the part of a lady named Kapiolani. A high chieftainess (women as well as men inherited rank in old Hawaii), Kapiolani became a Christian convert in the 1820s soon after the first boatload of missionaries arrived. To assist them in making other converts Kapiolani undertook to defy and humiliate Pele, and thus indirectly all of the local deities. Carrying a book given to her by the missionaries, she made a long journey on foot to the brink of the fire pit, announcing her iconoclastic intentions all the while. On Kilauea she flagrantly violated various taboos, going so far as to eat some *ohelo* berries without offering any to Pele. The *ohelo*, a relative of the huckleberry, grows in profusion near the volcano and was thought to be Pele's private property. Before eating any of the berries Hawaiians threw some into or towards the fire pit, saying, "Pele, here are your *ohelo*. I offer some to you; some I also eat." Failure to carry out this ritual would result in quick incineration.

Kapiolani was approached by a priestess from one of Pele's temples who showed her a letter of warning said to have been written by the goddess herself. "I too have a letter," said Kapiolani, taking the missionaries' book from under her arm and bravely reading aloud from it. Then she advanced to the edge of the lake of blazing lava, contemptuously tossed a few stones into it and made a speech, for which she may have received a little coaching. "Jehovah is my God. He kindled these fires. I fear not Pele. If I perish by the anger of Pele, then you may fear the power of Pele. But if I trust in Jehovah, and He shall keep me from the wrath of Pele when I break through her taboo, then you must fear and serve the Lord Jehovah. All the gods of Hawaii are in vain."

Nothing happened; there was no explosion, no fire fountain, nothing. Wrapped in her pride and her courage, Kapiolani walked home with her book. It was not a Bible, for she had not yet mastered the reading of complicated English. It was her spelling book.

Today any visitor may follow Kapiolani's path on Kilauea, more or less, and a great many do, particularly when Pele is having one of her frequent outbursts of temperament. Hawaiians attend volcanic eruptions with the enthusiasm of crowds descending on a major football game. They arrive by bus and by car, by public and private plane, often fetching drinks and sandwiches. When they reach Hawaii Volcanoes National Park they follow freshly set-out signs that say "To Eruption Site" just as motorists far to the east follow signs to the Yale Bowl.

The people of Hawaii flock to eruptions instead of fleeing from them because the local active volcanoes put on spectacular performances but never kill anyone; or hardly ever. The lava released from them, like all other lava, contains gas—chiefly water vapour, with small percentages of carbon dioxide, nitrogen, sulphur dioxide and several others. In volcanoes famous for deadly violence, such as Vesuvius or Krakatoa, the lava is sticky, viscous and likely to form solid plugs in the vents, trapping the gas and holding it under increasing pressure until it bursts forth in a terrific explosion. In Hawaiian volcanoes, however, the lava is much more fluid, of about the consistency and colour of thick tomato soup. Gas escapes from it easily, often whooshing upwards in great fire fountains, but without major explosions. Rarely, a sudden draining of ground water into a hot volcanic vent may produce a series of steam blasts, but there has been only one such event in this century, at Kilauea in 1924. It killed one man, who ignored advice to stay away from the area and was hit by a flying rock. Ordinarily Hawaiian eruptions produce boiling lakes of lava, rivers, gushers and geysers of incandescent liquid stone spurting as high as 1,900 feet into the air. As the lava spreads away from the vents it gradually cools and solidifies, often destroying roads, crops and houses.

Highly fluid lava may flow as far as 30 miles before cooling into immobility or running into the ocean, and for short distances on steep slopes it may move as fast as 35 mph. Often, however, the lava partially hardens, acquiring a clinkery, rubbly surface and a dense semisolid core that may take all day to travel half a mile. Both the slow

and fast flows are fascinating to watch but the fast ones create by far
the more interesting forms. The top and sides of a rapidly running
stream may congeal into a hard black crust, making a tube within which
the lava continues to flow like water in a pipe. When the supply is shut
off the liquid drains out of the tube, which may later be buried beneath
succeeding flows to become a tunnel within a growing mountain. Some
of the lava tubes in Kilauea and Mauna Loa are as large as subway tunnels; the best known of them, the Thurston lava tube in the National
Park, has been fitted with electric lights and accommodates hundreds
of strollers every day.

At times fluid lava may pour through a forest, hardening around the
cool, moist trunks of trees as it passes. The heat sets the trees afire and
the wood is burned out. The ashes disappear, leaving hollow pillars
with moulds of the long-dead trees inside them. If the flow does not
drain away but remains to cover the forest, the tree moulds appear as
holes in the ground.

Hawaiian lava tends to cover broad areas with thin flows, many of
them only a few feet thick. Mauna Loa, at nearly 14,000 feet above sea
level and 30,000 feet above the ocean floor, has thus been built up of
thousands of layers. It has no sharply defined peak, but is shaped like
an inverted circular shield. Both Mauna Loa and Kilauea, which is several thousand feet lower and built against the side of its larger brother,
are in fact called shield volcanoes. Their long, flattened profiles contrast with the steep truncated cones that come to mind when one thinks
of volcanoes such as Shasta or Fuji. However, the gentle curves of the
Hawaiian volcanoes disguise astonishing bulk. Mauna Loa, with a volume of 10,000 cubic miles, is by far the largest volcanic mountain on
earth, a hundred times larger than either Shasta or Fuji.

The principal vents of Kilauea and Mauna Loa are at their summits,
where signs of forthcoming eruptions often first appear. Sometimes the
eruptions are confined there, but frequently the lava issues from a zone
of rifts (or fissures) on the flank of the mountain 5, 10 or even 25 miles
away. Both volcanoes have two major rift zones, lines of weakness
trending generally southwest and east, that are marked by craters, frac-
tures, cinder cones and recent lava flows. In the southwest rift zone of
Kilauea there is an enormous fissure called the Great Crack, which extends without interruption for 14 miles. In places it is as much as 50
feet wide, and a man can climb down into it for 60 or 70 feet before it becomes too narrow for further descent. From the air the rift zones appear

like battlefields where armies have been fighting with flame throwers: black, melted slopes strewn with scorched pillboxes, smouldering forts, charred forests, trenches oozing steam and fumes. Yet, wherever the lava has not flowed in recent times, plants and trees have returned.

To the old Hawaiians the legends of Pele were all the more real because eruptions of lava might, and did, suddenly occur at any time anywhere, near a village, in a taro patch or on a hill that was good for sledging. When such things happened it was easy enough for witnesses to recall that there had been an ugly old woman or a beautiful young one prowling somewhere in the neighbourhood; there usually is. But today the unpredictability of eruptions has been largely eliminated. Scientists at the Hawaiian Volcano Observatory, perched almost on the rim of the main vent of Kilauea, have learned to forecast—within reasonable limits—when another outbreak is likely to occur. Kilauea is a fine volcano to study. Indeed there is no other on earth that lends itself quite so well, in accessibility, docility and frequency of action, to the purpose. There has been a volcano observatory at Kilauea since 1912, established through the efforts of the late, brilliant geologist Thomas A. Jaggar. It was originally supported by M.I.T. and by scientifically inclined Hawaiian businessmen; today it is maintained by the U.S. Geological Survey.

The general mechanics of Kilauea and Mauna Loa, although not all the important details, are fairly well understood by now. A complex mixture of melted rock and gases, called magma when it is below the surface and lava when it emerges, originates about 40 miles underground. Because it is lighter than the solid rock pressing down around it, it is squeezed upwards through vertical channels and accumulates in chambers or reservoirs only two or three miles below the summits of the volcanoes. When the pressure within the reservoirs becomes great enough—whoosh! Before an eruption the summit of a volcano inflates or swells, often by as much as four or five feet, sometimes in a few days and sometimes over a period of months. The swelling is imperceptible to the eye because it takes place all across the top of a huge, flattened dome; but instruments at the volcano observatory can measure it with great precision. Surveyors' levels determine how much the ground rises or falls. Geodimeters, using laser beams, measure changes in distance between various points. Tiltmeters, anchored firmly in the mountain, can translate the smallest motion into a variable electric current that is then translated back into the motion of a stylus on a graph in the laboratory. The accuracy of the tiltmeters has given rise to a local figure of speech that, however extreme it sounds, is true enough: if you have a steel girder one mile long, and you raise one end of it high enough to slip a nickel under it, the instruments can measure the tilt.

A network of seismographs, which record earth tremors not only beneath the volcanoes but throughout the island and under the surrounding sea, provides a good deal more information for the scientists. As a rule several dozen quakes are recorded each day, although occasionally there are "swarms" of a few hundred or even 2,000 to 3,000 in 24 hours. Only rarely, however, is a quake strong enough to be felt throughout the island. Still, the depth and duration of the seismic patterns are revealing, and there is a particular sort of record that can raise the hair on the back of any geologist's neck no matter how many seismographs he has looked at in his lifetime. That is harmonic tremor, a steady, heavy pulsing or pounding that indicates that magma is coursing through underground conduits on the way to the surface. The signature of harmonic tremor on a seismogram is unmistakably distinct from the blips made by ordinary quakes; it goes on and on, for hours or months, a rhythmic, wide swinging of the stylus not unlike an exercise in the old Palmer Method of penmanship.

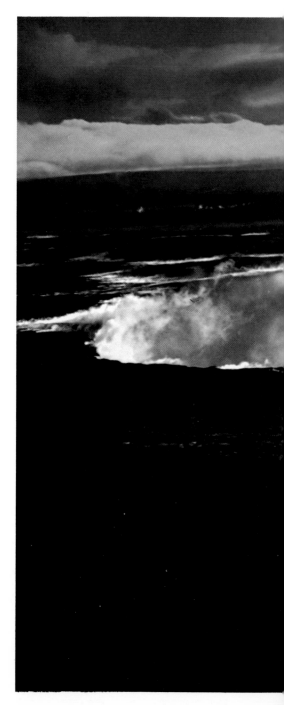

Although the volcanologists in Hawaii have learned much about the prediction of eruptions, they can do little but offer suggestions as to how to cope with the whopper that seems likely to come—not necessarily tomorrow but, as geological time goes, pretty soon. The third largest city and seaport in the state, Hilo, with a population in the mid-1970s of about 30,000, is located some 40 miles from the summit of Mauna Loa in line with the course of many past lava flows. And when the volcano erupts it discharges almost unbelievable quantities of lava —the flow of 1950, luckily on the southwest rather than the northeast rift that faces Hilo, was on the order of one thousand million tons. On several occasions lava from Mauna Loa has menaced Hilo—the flow of 1881 came within a mile of the centre of the town and there were serious threats in 1855, 1899, 1935 and 1942. The eruption of 1942 received no notice in the press—the Japanese had attacked Pearl Harbor only four months before, the islands were under a nightly blackout, and there seemed no reason to inform enemy submarine captains that they could find Hawaii the way Moses found the promised land, by following a pillar of smoke by day and of fire by night.

The eruption of 1942 began in late April and by May 1 the lava was only 12 miles from Hilo, advancing at 300 to 500 feet an hour on a front

Vapours released by lava rise from the Halemaumau fire pit, a 3,200-foot-wide crater contained within the sunken top of Kilauea Volcano.

half a mile wide. It seemed about to inundate an aqueduct and a main highway, vital for military purposes, and its approach to the city was particularly alarming to residents because of the noise that accompanied it. The flow was advancing through swampy jungle, where in the clouds of smoke and brown steam could be heard what sounded like a rolling artillery barrage: pockets of methane gas, generated in the decomposing vegetation, exploding.

Volcanologists and local authorities made up their minds to meet violence with violence, or at any rate with the comprehensible, almost quaint sort of violence that was available in those days. Once before, in 1935, the U.S. Army Air Corps had used old Keystone bombers to try to alter (without much success) the course of a lava flow headed towards Hilo, and now the scientists called on the Army again. Several 500-pound bombs were dropped high on the rift zone at points where the flow might have been turned aside and there was, briefly, a minor diversion. However, by good fortune the eruption soon ceased of its own accord. There was no evidence that the bombs had done any good. The question remains open. If Hilo is threatened again it is quite possible that the Navy or the Air Force may be asked to use the remarkably accurate "smart bombs" developed during the war in Vietnam. An alternative defence for Hilo, seriously proposed by one of the most respected geologists in Hawaii, is to build a wall 17 miles long and 25 feet high across the rift zone to deflect the lava away from the city.

Unlike Mauna Loa, Kilauea menaces no cities because there are none within its reach, although in 1960, without loss of life, it wiped out the small town of Kapoho along with some papaya groves, sugar cane and fields of cultivated orchids. The eruption took place more than 20 miles from Kilauea's summit, but it is at the summit that any close look at the volcano should begin.

In the top of Kilauea's flattened dome there is a roughly oval, sunken area, typical of shield volcanoes, called a caldera. Created by the collapse of the interior of the mountain, the caldera is about two miles across and has clifflike walls that plunge as much as 400 feet down to a flat floor 2,600 acres in area. When he first saw this sunken plain Mark Twain remarked that all the armies of Russia could camp there and have room to spare. The shape of the caldera raises an odd image in the mind of a visitor. It appears that the volcano contains a gigantic cylinder and piston: at the moment the piston is on the downstroke, creating the caldera, but on the upstroke it will rise flush with the surrounding area and all will be level again. The caldera floor is covered with fairly recent flows of lava, poured out at intervals in the last 150 years, dark grey or black, dull or shiny, smooth or wrinkled as the light chances to strike it. In the southwestern quadrant of the caldera there is a circular crater more than half a mile and (as of early 1973) 300 feet deep. This is the great fire pit, the home of Pele and for countless years the centre of action on Kilauea.

The fire pit is called Halemaumau, the House of the Ferns, probably in reference to the tall *amaumau* ferns that grow near by. The ferns were once used by Hawaiians to make temporary shelters when they came to pay their respects to Pele. The name persists, although since the 19th Century more substantial material has been used to construct guesthouses on the rim of the caldera. In 1866 a wooden hotel, Volcano House, was erected for the tourist trade and was visited by Twain, who was then a 31-year-old correspondent for the *Sacramento Union*. After various remodellings and rebuildings Volcano House still stands above the dark volcanic depression; visitors today stare out of its windows at Halemaumau smouldering below.

Not far away, in another building even closer to the fire pit, volcanologists stare out of *their* windows at the rising smoke and steam, or read the seismograms and tiltmeter reports that are constantly wired into their quarters. Halemaumau, despite its ominous appearance, no longer contains the lake of molten lava that made it world-famous for a century prior to 1924. Tourists used to peer down into it, seeing—as did Mark Twain—a great cauldron "ringed and streaked and striped with a thousand branching streams of liquid and gorgeously brilliant fire! It looked like a colossal railway map of the state of Massachusetts done in chain-lighting on a midnight sky. Imagine it—imagine a coal-black sky shivered into a tangled network of angry fire!" Other visitors saw other visions, perhaps depending on the states they came from or what preachers they had lately been listening to, but everyone saw something astonishing. At times the lake rose and overflowed onto the caldera floor; at times black rafts of hardened lava drifted on its crimson surface, or dozens of fountains leaped and splashed there. But suddenly in 1924, at the time of the steam explosion mentioned earlier, the lake disappeared and one of the great sights of the earth vanished. Since then it has returned only at brief, infrequent intervals.

Visitors are politely discouraged from entering the observatory, although they may look through a window at a row of working seismographs that the volcanologists have placed close behind the glass.

Dead ohia trees, victims of hot cinders, ash and sparks from the 1959-1960 eruption of Kilauea Volcano, loom over a slope of Kilauea Iki Crater, where all vegetation was destroyed—an area now aptly called Devastation Trail.

Visitors may also wander across the slopes of Kilauea, following paths marked by stakes, cairns and bits of bright plastic tape set out by rangers of the National Park Service. Although the rangers' prime consideration is safety, they will often, when conditions are right, allow sightseers to walk to the brink of a crater where newly erupted lava is boiling below. However, it is the scientists who go out almost daily into the unmarked, steaming, boot-scorching wilderness, and the scientists who occasionally get blistered.

Men who choose to study volcanoes at close range are not ribbon clerks. They are an unusual breed. Dr. Donald Peterson, the scientist in charge of the observatory, has been scorched more than once, and perhaps a glance at a typical scorching will serve somewhat to describe him. A while ago he was asked, as a favour to a fellow scientist, to provide a sample of fresh lava that had been contaminated as little as possible by contact with organic matter—that is, a bit of lava that had never flowed along the mortal earth or even remained long exposed to the spore- and germ-rich air. It seemed to Peterson, who is a trim, athletic man in his late forties, that the way to obtain such a sample was to pick it up with tongs immediately after it popped out of a volcanic vent. Lava often emerges in half-melted blobs that sail 10 to 20 feet into the air, fall, and build up formations called spatter cones. One variety of blob, because of its striking resemblance to the genuine article, is called a cow-dung bomb. While Dr. Peterson was searching with his tongs for a suitably fresh blob, venturing courageously close to the active cone, a large number of them suddenly flew out of it all at once. As he turned and ran, a ball of lava hit him on the back of the neck and fell down inside his shirt, causing what he calls "a little discomfort". However, he persisted in his attempts with the tongs, finally snatched up a likely specimen, clapped it into a container and sent the sample off.

On a midsummer morning Dr. Peterson invited me to take a walk with him out into the east rift zone of Kilauea where an eruption was in progress. It was a lovely day for a stroll, as Beelzebub might have said, with just the tiniest seasoning of sulphur in the air and a nice showing of harmonic tremor on the seismograph. Because the eruption site was several miles from the observatory, we covered much of the distance in a jeep, accompanied by a young geologist from the National Aeronautics and Space Administration, Grant Heiken. NASA is interested in hot places and may establish its own volcano laboratory in Central America. Heiken, lending a hand with Peterson's equipment, was carrying a newly designed 10-foot-long thermocouple, a device for measuring temperatures. When we came to a convenient pool of molten lava Peterson was going to stick the thermocouple into it.

On the way to the eruption site Peterson talked briefly about the function of the observatory, which does a good deal more than study volcanoes. It co-operates with physicists investigating magnetism and isotopes, with botanists who are interested in the return of vegetation to devastated areas, and with astronomers studying gases by spectroscope. At the moment there is some interest in the nonpollutive production of electric power by using the volcanoes as sources of heat, but many problems must be solved before this source is successfully tapped. A power plant requires a good deal of fresh water for the generation of steam, but not much is available locally. The volcanic rock is so porous that water sinks into it quickly. Although there are many streams, there are few fresh-water lakes in the entire state of Hawaii. Even if ample water were available for geothermal power, Peterson says, the location of a plant in an active volcanic area is no casual matter. The source of heat beneath the plant might migrate to some other spot, making the plant useless, or perhaps a new eruption might bury the plant in lava or reduce it to a heap of cinders.

After driving for about 10 miles along the east rift we reached a place where the jeep could go no farther; the road was blocked by hardened billows of recent lava. Behind us there was a fairly luxuriant growth of trees, bushes and grass; ahead there was only a dead, solidified ocean, gunmetal in colour but streaked here and there with ochre and dry lizard grey. On the surface of the lava there was a sheen created by innumerable flat threads of volcanic glass—it resembles fibreglass in appearance and materializes on the crust as it cools. About half a mile distant against the sky faint puffs of smoke marked the vent from which the lava had poured.

A foot trail, indicated by white metal rods jammed into crevices, led across the stone ocean to the summit of the shield, which was about 300 feet high and a couple of square miles in area. A good many people had walked along the trail before us and their feet had worn away the threads of glass, making the trail dull black in contrast to the shiny lava near by, and quieter to step on. Whenever a man happened to wander off the worn path the glass threads made a faint, crisp, grinding noise beneath his boots. (Mark Twain, walking across the floor of the Kilauea caldera at night, lost his way and got back on the trail only after a companion relocated it by sound.) As we walked, Peterson remarked that the shield, called Mauna Ulu (Growing Mountain), was the largest new volcanic land form to arise in the United States in many centuries, and that it had been created by the longest flank eruption in the recorded history of Kilauea. It began in May 1969, continued for two and a half years, paused briefly and resumed in February 1972.

It was an easy walk to the low summit of Mauna Ulu. Little gusts of heated air and steam emerged from cracks in the lava, tinged with faint whiffs of gas. City people walking over subway gratings in the winter encounter much the same warmth and smell, although what is running underground in Mauna Ulu is hotter than the A train to Harlem. At the top of the shield behind a rope barrier a score of visitors were peering down into the crater. Near by, seated on a lump of lava that suggested a throne, sat a guardian park ranger. He was not wearing a Smokey-the-Bear hat but a helmet and seemed a figure from Milton or Dante, staring hard at the visitors and occasionally cautioning them with his voice or merely with a flick of his eyes. Several of the visitors had cameras and were pressing against the rope, within three or four feet of the brink, to take pictures. The crater at this point was not very wide, perhaps only 70 yards, and about 25 yards deep. Heavy smoke drifted inside it, parting at times to reveal a pond of glowing orange lava below. The lava appeared to be welling up at one side of the pond and disappearing at the other, in steady circulation although the level of the pond remained constant. In the past several months the pond level had fluctuated greatly, the lava sometimes sinking to a depth of 60 yards below the crater rim and sometimes rising to overflow the spot on which we were standing.

Peterson exchanged greetings with the ranger and then, passing a sign that said, "Danger. Do not pass," set out in an easterly direction along the rim of the crater. He moved briskly and easily although he was wearing a 40-pound backpack full of instruments, cameras, heavy gloves, first-aid equipment, rock hammers and other geologist's gear. The crater, or trench, was about a third of a mile in length and maintained its 70-yard width throughout that distance. Peterson occasionally glanced down into it but noted little that had changed since his last visit. Fumes were rising from the depths but we rarely caught a whiff of them; the trade-wind breeze, coming steadily from the northeast, pushed them away. In any case they would not have been troublesome because we were out in the open where the fresh air could dilute them. "A while ago," Peterson said, "I saw a bat fly in there and die."

Hawaiian bats sometimes sleep in crannies in the walls of craters, and when they emerge they may be engulfed by rising gases. "This one came out a hole," Peterson went on, "fluttered for a few seconds, fell into the lava and winked out like a match." The same fate sometimes overtakes the white-tailed tropic birds that nest in the walls of the Kilauea caldera. During an eruption in 1969 several of these large birds, which have wingspreads of three feet or more, flew into fume clouds, lost consciousness and fell like meteors.

Leaving Mauna Ulu, Peterson continued east towards the site of Alae, which until the current eruption had been one of several deep pit craters that mark the upper part of Kilauea's east rift zone. During the Mauna Ulu eruption, however, Alae had been filled with new lava, drained, refilled, drained and refilled still again. And even now it was filled to the brim and overflowing with lava that was creating a new shield where the crater once had been. As we climbed its gentle slope I could see above us small clots of soupy liquid flying into the air.

At the summit of Alae's shield stood a spatter cone perhaps 30 feet high and 50 feet in diameter at its base. From a vent near the top of the cone came a deep sloshing, woofing noise, the sound of an enormous, infernal piece of plumbing, and out of the base of the cone, not its top, gushed the lava. It was bright yellow-orange and moving with great speed, a torrential river compressed within close banks. In a short distance the banks flared out and the lava poured into a large lake that was contained within a recently hardened levee all around the summit. Peterson walked towards the sideways-gushing fountain, studying it with a pleased eye. I asked him what he estimated the volume of flow to be and he began to work out the problem in his head, staring at the gusher to gauge its diameter and speed.

The gunmetal lava underfoot was hot. The heat penetrated the thick soles of my boots but it was not strong enough to make them smoke. A good deal of heat was radiating from the wide-open hydrant of lava, too, but it was not unpleasant at a distance of 30 or 40 feet. The surface of the lake, which was several hundred yards long, was covered with a thin, fragile black crust. Choppy waves constantly broke the crust, revealing the brilliant liquid beneath, and in several places low fountains, 5 or 10 feet in height, spurted and splashed. The level of the lake was only a few feet below its levee and visibly rising. It appeared that it would overflow, somewhere, within the next few minutes.

Peterson completed his calculation. The flow from the gusher was about 40 cubic metres or 1,000 gallons per second, only a trickle in comparison with the major outpourings, sometimes a hundred times greater,

64/

that Kilauea occasionally releases. Still, 1,000 gallons of hot lava per second is a considerable amount. I did a quick calculation of my own and concluded that it would completely fill a large church—say, the Presbyterian church where as a lad I learned about infant damnation —in one minute. The lake was also being fed from underground sources, probably being connected by tubes with the crater of Mauna Ulu. Peterson glanced hopefully in various directions, looking for a spot where a breakthrough and overflow might occur. Our own elevation was about three feet above lake level but there were other places where the lava was lapping only a few inches from the top of the levee. Peninsulas and bays made it impossible for us to see the entire shore, however; we were thus unprepared for the breakthrough when it came. The level of the lake simply began to drop; somewhere close by but out of sight a stream of lava had begun to pour down the side of the shield.

Instead of walking around the summit to find the break Peterson went downhill towards the base. It was possible that the break might suddenly widen, causing problems for pedestrians in the neighbourhood, and Peterson wanted to be well removed from it. He would approach the stream of lava from a lower level and from the side. The surface of the shield, like that of Mauna Ulu, was covered with glossy black billows. But here no one had staked out a trail around the treacherous spots. Many of the billows were hollow, their interiors having drained away, and though they appeared solid they were only brittle crusts a few inches thick. As we walked on them the billows cracked and sagged. Sometimes they broke completely, dropping a man up to his knees in sharp-edged shards that clattered and tinkled. A continual breaking-crockery noise accompanied us down the slope of the shield.

At the bottom Peterson headed east again, his backpack joggling as he hopped along the lava. He has a doctorate in geology from Stanford, has worked for the U.S. Geological Survey for 20 years, and is of course a public employee. As I hurried to keep up with him it struck me that the taxpayers were certainly getting their money's worth from him. Soon he stopped short and pointed out into the sloping field of lava in front of us. "There."

At first I saw only the black, frozen sea, but as I stared it suddenly became apparent that a long strip of the sea was moving. In the middle distance, bounded in the foreground and background by fixed, seemingly firm banks, a stream of lava was flowing downhill from right to left. There were small streaks of orange in it but in the main it was crusted

Lava from a volcano can take many different forms, depending on its temperature and composition when it emerges into the air. The common variety the Hawaiians call aa, consisting of large amounts of gas in a relatively cool (1,000°F. to 1,500°F.) mixture of rough, clinkery chunks of basalt, moves quite slowly but can cover extensive areas. At higher temperatures (1,600°F. to 2,000°F.) lava pours out in a liquid form called pahoehoe, which contains fewer and smaller gas bubbles, and travels farther and faster than aa. Lava also occurs in rarer forms such as obsidian and Pele's hair–varieties of volcanic glass that cool and harden in shimmering strands on the lava surface.

GLOWING AA

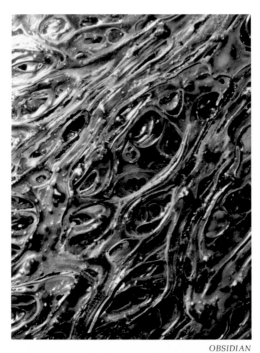

OBSIDIAN

COOLED PAHOEHOE

PELE'S HAIR (CENTRE)

over, distinguishable from the hard lava on both sides of it only by the fact that it was in motion. The motion was steady and sedate, only a mile or two an hour on the gentle slope. Strange shapes swept silently along like black ice floes on a black river, or like figures and floats in a truly Godforsaken parade.

Peterson, full of enthusiasm, headed for the river with all deliberate speed. As we approached it, circling the lower part of the shield, we could look up and see the break in the levee of the lake perched above us. In truth it was not a break but merely the lowest spot in the levee over which the lava was pouring. That was the manner in which the shield grew: the lake rose and fell, constantly building its levee higher and higher, and at intervals it poured over the low spots. Sometimes several flows would come over the levee at once, radiating like spokes from a wheel hub. Peterson knew about that, and as we approached the river he mentioned the possibility. In the next few minutes, he said, he would be busy testing the thermocouple and would not have time to keep his eye on the levee, which was perhaps 20 yards above us and 200 yards away. Would someone please glance up occasionally, and let him know if a new flow of lava started to come down behind us? His words were, "It is not a good idea to be caught between two flows of lava". I volunteered to look up at the levee once in a while.

The lava at the edge of the river was sluggish, cooling and building banks. Its crust, however, was very thin and flexible. Peterson found a convenient place to test the thermocouple and, helped by Heiken, the geologist from NASA, prepared to do so. The principle of the device, long known, is this: when two dissimilar metals such as copper and iron are joined and simultaneously heated, a tiny electric current is generated. The current can be run through an ammeter and expressed on a gauge as temperature. The particular instrument that Peterson was testing resembled a long curtain rod with a meter connected by wires to one end; the other end was to be thrust into the lava.

Peterson put on a pair of gloves and, shielding his face from the heat with his forearm, advanced to the riverbank. The thermocouple rod was 10 feet long but its effective length was somewhat shorter because he had to stick it well into the lava to get a fair temperature reading. I moved up close to him for a few moments to feel the heat but then retreated, dropping a plastic ball-point pen I had been using to take notes. As it lay on the hard lava where Peterson was standing the pen turned into a piece of macaroni.

As Peterson held the rod tip in the molten lava, Heiken, some distance behind him, read the gauge and called out the temperature in degrees Fahrenheit. "1,600 . . . 1,650 . . . 1,675 . . . 1,700."

Petersen withdrew the rod and stepped back. Because the rod was relatively cool a blob of lava had hardened around the end of it, making the temperature reading inaccurate. With the blunt end of his geologist's hammer he carefully knocked off the blob, and then decided that he would stick the rod into a lava toe. Soft, liquid lava, of the sort we were dealing with, advances by thrusting forward rounded pillow-like protuberances called toes, not human in appearance but such as might be seen on an enormous black gingerbread man oozing across a cookie sheet. Peterson bent over a toe, which appeared to have an inch-thick crust on it, and struck it with the pointed end of his hammer. He poked a hole in it from which several spurts of orange lava flew up. A pea-sized drop hit him on the back of the wrist and fell down inside his glove. He quickly shook it out, muttering, and thrust the end of the thermocouple into the hole. In a few moments Heiken reported that the needle on the temperature gauge had touched 2,000°F.

Peterson had only one more task: he wanted to collect a sample of fresh lava, and so he stuck the pointed end of his hammer into the hole in the toe and hooked out a red-hot lump. He allowed it to cool briefly on the hammer, then popped it into a little cloth bag and put the bag into his backpack. As we walked and floundered across the hollow billows on the way back to the jeep he said, "A while ago I failed to let a sample cool long enough and it set fire to my pack. Embarrassing."

After we returned to the volcano laboratory I took leave of Dr. Peterson and drove down to Hilo, wondering where I would place a 17-mile-long 25-foot wall if someone asked me to build one. I was travelling alone, on my way to Hilo airport to catch a plane to another island. On the road I passed an old lady who had a flower stand, really only a table with some local orchids and anthuriums in tin cans. I had no use for flowers, not then, but she was staring at me with an odd expression. Although she was not ugly she was scarcely beautiful and she was in a sense asking me a favour. It dawned on me that a few flowers might not be a bad investment, so I bought some, and my car got all the way to Hilo without catching fire.

NATURE WALK / **In Kipuka Puaulu**

PHOTOGRAPHS BY DAVID CAVAGNARO

On the slopes of Mauna Loa the overlapping and intertwining flows of lava have created islands called *kipuka*—the Hawaiian word for an opening. Sometimes *kipuka* form small hills, but more often they are pockets in the mountainside surrounded by more recent lava flows. Within the *kipuka*, plants have escaped the devastation that has swept past them on all sides; birds and butterflies find refuge there; and in the green shadows are echoes and fragrances of a time long vanished.

One of the most luxuriant of the *kipuka* on Mauna Loa lies at an altitude of 4,000 feet. It is called Puaulu, a combination of the words *pua*, which means both flower and a collection of things bound together, and *ulu*, to grow. Puaulu is so lush because it lies in the path of warm moist air that sweeps up the mountain from Hilo, at the base of Mauna Loa's fellow volcano, Kilauea.

Puaulu comprises 100 acres, which is large as *kipuka* go; many are only a few dozen square yards in size. It is roughly oval, with a trail that makes a loop of about a mile around its edge. Its age cannot be accurately determined but its huge *koa* and *ohia lehua* trees, some of them standing in small glades and others in patch-es of dense climax forest, are part of a community that has been undisturbed for hundreds of years—perhaps since the birth of Christ.

It takes about an hour to walk around Puaulu, allowing time for pauses to look and smell and listen, but even a dozen circuits of it reveal only a fraction of the *kipuka*'s varied attractions. The rangers of Hawaii Volcanoes National Park have explored it many times and still consider themselves to be merely acquainted with the place, and not thoroughly knowledgeable about it. In fact, several basic studies of Puaulu remain to be made, to discover more about the evolution and inter-relationships that distinguish this isolated community.

However, it is not a scientific interest that moves a man on first approaching Puaulu, but a sense of wonder and even of mystery. To me the trees and plants, though not at first glance dramatically different from those of the American mainland, were still unfamiliar enough on a recent visit to make me stop and stare. My thoughts then turned to the Hawaiians themselves, who enjoyed a greenwood instead of a metallic culture, who intimately knew these plants and put them to shrewd or curious uses that have now slipped almost beyond memory.

The way to the *kipuka* passes over lava flows of recent centuries where the topsoil is still shallow and the vegetation stunted. Here and there on the rocks patches of grey beard-like lichen grow, slowly and invisibly breaking down the stone into

PIONEER LICHEN ON LAVA ROCK

earth by means of minute amounts of organic acids that the lichen secretes both when it photosynthesizes and when it decomposes. Entering the *kipuka* I passed quickly into the cool shade of a mixed forest. For the rest of the walk, save in a few small, grassy, sunlit areas, I was enclosed in the woods and saw no large vistas. I could fix my attention on the greenery around me.

The ground cover alongside the

KOA (LEFT) AND OHIA TREES

OAK FERN IN THE OPEN FOREST

trail was thick with delicate oak ferns—their fronds characteristically thinner at the base than in the middle—and also with crane's-bills, otherwise known as wild geraniums. Overhead were the intermingling branches of soapberry trees and Hawaiian olives, whose fruit is inedible but whose hardwood was once used for spears and adze handles. I had the good luck to glimpse a Kamehameha butterfly perched on a knee-high bracken fern. Highly coloured, with a wingspan of about four inches, the Kamehameha is found in the forests of all the major Hawaiian Islands—but nowhere else in the world.

A few of the plants visible from the trail are familiar to mainland gardeners. The broad-leaved ti is widely known for its decorative qualities; its flowers, appearing in spring, grow in branched clusters at least a foot

A KAMEHAMEHA BUTTERFLY

long, bearing half-inch-long white buds tinged pale purple. In times past, the Hawaiians found the ti useful as well as decorative. The leaves were used as thatch, stitched together to make skirts, or wrapped around food that was to be cooked or stored. In those innocent days the Hawaiians brewed a weak alcoholic drink

from the ti's thick roots, which are rich in sugar. But around 1800, white men showed them how to make stills from blubber kettles and musket barrels, and the ti became the source of a skull-popping rumlike concoction called okolehao. A civilized version of the liquor is sold in Honolulu liquor stores today.

A Nut for Burning

Near the ti plants along the trail was a kukui, or candlenut, tree. It too looked familiar—in this case deceptively so. With the sun shining down through them, the leaves were shaped much like the leaves of mainland maples. Totally unlike the maple, however, the tree bears a nut that used to be burned for illumination—hence the name. The nut was also put to other purposes, including ritualistic retribution against criminals. Scattered in a fire kindled for

A DECORATIVE, POTENT TI PLANT

LEAVES OF THE CANDLENUT TREE

POMPON BLOOMS OF THE OHIA TREE

the occasion by priests, the kernels of the nut furnished magic that was guaranteed—provided the ceremony was accompanied by the proper incantation—to make a thief give himself up, on pain of certain death.

Some of the towering *ohia lehua* trees beside the trail were tilted at fantastic angles by the wind but still thriving, in full bloom with brilliant clustered scarlet flowers. The *ohia* has shallow roots, a disadvantage at times of hurricane, but in other ways a source of strength: since the seeds of the tree are light and easily airborne, the *ohia* is a pioneer among plants in revegetating newly lava-covered areas. Sailing out of the *kipuka*, the seeds lodge in lava crevices where only shallow-rooted plants may take hold; in time these

crack the stone and make room for other plants that delve more deeply.

Common throughout all Polynesia, the *ohia* as it appears in Hawaii is remarkably varied in form. There are so many subspecies that it is impossible to classify them all. In the Kau region, a stone desert on the southeast side of Mauna Loa, the *ohia* may be a tiny shrub only a foot tall but fully mature, producing seeds and beautiful crimson pompon blooms.

In such inhospitable places the young *ohia* may hitch a ride on an even earlier arrival—the sadleria fern. Airborne *ohia* seeds may take root in the branches of the sadleria, extend their roots earthwards and eventually strangle the fern. This ability of the *ohia* to grow as an epiphyte, or air plant, led the early

AN OHIA TREE TILTED BY THE WIND

BRACKET FUNGUS ON OHIA BARK

Hawaiians to think of the fern as the parent of the tree. In Kipuka Puaulu the oldest *ohia*, with their bark encrusted at intervals on the trunk by bracket fungus resembling outsized clams, reach heights of about 100 feet. *Ohia* wood is dark red, handsomely grained and tough. From it the Hawaiians made planks that were pegged as gunwales on their big dugout canoes. Rubbing against these hard boards, the relatively easily made paddles wore out, while the softer sides of the laboriously hollowed boats went unscathed.

A Medicinal Relic

Beside the trail, both on the ground and in clefts in the trees, grew a strange primitive plant called *moa* by the Hawaiians and *Psilotum nudum* by botanists. Its stems are triangular, its scales grow no more than one-eighth of an inch long; in its general appearance—somewhat like seaweed—it resembles certain other plant species so long extinct that they are known today only as fossils. By boiling the *moa* the Hawaiians produced a medicinal tea that they found useful in curing thrush, a

A PRIMITIVE, MEDICINAL MOA PLANT

fungus infection of the mouth common in infants. They also employed the tea as a laxative, while to combat diarrhoea they swallowed the *moa*'s powdery spores.

About halfway around the loop I came upon a rare *holei* tree, a native plant with boldly decorative leathery leaves. Near by were a few dwarfed but hardy *hapuu* tree ferns, which ordinarily thrive better at lower altitudes, where they reach heights of 35 feet or more.

At several points the edge of the trail was adorned with the fleshy white fruit of the *mamaki*, a large shrub about 15 feet high that was once among the Hawaiians' most prized plants. Its inner bark furnished a durable cloth, resembling cotton, that was made into skirts for women and loincloths for men.

LEAVES OF THE RARE HOLEI TREE

Also thriving in the *kipuka* was the *koali*, a common morning-glory whose pale violet blooms form a startlingly delicate contrast to the coarse leaves of the vine on which they grow. Known in Hawaiian legend as a source of rope, the vine is celebrated in even older Polynesian folklore as the source of the human race; its juice once produced worms that the Creator, Tangaloa, transformed into people and endowed with intelligence.

In experimenting with the properties of the plants and trees in their islands the Hawaiians always had an eye for any amusement they could derive. Such was the case with the *papala*, which I recognized beside the trail by the tiny flowers that stippled the tips of its branches. The *papala* supplied the Hawaiians with fireworks. The wood of the tree is very light and flammable; coated with oil, it burns briskly. Discovering this, the Hawaiians fashioned long *papala* spears, set them alight and hurled them at night from high cliffs above the water. To the delight of watchers floating in their canoes below, the spears would sail great distances on the trade winds—like a swarm of comets in the dark sky —before sputtering into the sea.

A White Strawberry

As I reached the open forest at the halfway mark on the trail, the spacing of the trees enabled me to get a better look at the ground cover, and I was struck by its great variety. Among the most widespread of the ground huggers was a strawberry bearing a white fruit. Though not a

/75

STEMS AND FLOWERS OF THE FLAMMABLE PAPALA

THE MAMAKI: SOURCE OF NATIVE CLOTH

A HARDY HAPUU TREE FERN

DELICATE KOALI MORNING-GLORIES

native of Hawaii—it originated in Europe and North America—the plant is strange, with its pale berry that never reddens even when ripe. Interspersed among the strawberry plants was the luxuriant foliage of the *kopiko*, a member of the coffee family that accounts, along with its 10 or so Hawaiian relatives, for a large percentage of the native forest vegetation. Another somewhat larger ground cover, formerly considered sacred to the goddess Pele, was the shrubby *ohelo*, which bears berries the Hawaiians also considered good to eat; they could not eat the fruit, however, until they had propitiated the fire goddess by throwing *ohelo* branches, berries attached, into the lava pit of Kilauea.

A Majestic Giant

Past its midpoint the loop trail on Puaulu has a short spur that leads out almost to the edge of the *kipuka*, within sight of the newer lava that surrounds it. There in lone majesty stands a giant *koa* tree, 10 feet in diameter at its base. It is doubtless hundreds of years old, but there is no way of knowing its precise age. In tropical and subtropical latitudes trees do not produce well-defined growth rings that can be counted. In attempting to determine their age from samples withdrawn from their trunks by core bits, botanists can only make estimates. The huge *koa* tree I saw had a many-branched trunk, but the species also produces trees with one trunk of great girth. It was from these that Hawaiian craftsmen fashioned their canoes.

The making of canoes, particularly

WHITE HAWAIIAN STRAWBERRIES

the large vessels designed for war or long ocean voyages, was accompanied by a good deal of ceremony and prayer. When a Hawaiian located a suitable *koa* tree in the forest he told a *kahuna* (priest) about it, and the *kahuna* went into a temple to sleep in the hope of having an auspicious dream. If in his dream he saw a naked man or woman the tree was considered rotten and unfit; but if the person was well clothed the tree was deemed suitable. Other signs being propitious, the priest then went into the woods and cut down the *koa* with a stone axe. Finished canoes were very narrow, between one and three feet in width, but as much as 100 feet long and 10 feet deep.

The *koa* tree also furnished wood for Hawaiians' surfboards, which

THE UBIQUITOUS KOPIKO

were a good deal larger than those in use today—in the collection of boards in the Bishop Museum in Honolulu there is one 16 feet long.

From the giant *koa* tree the Puaulu trail curves gently to the right towards where it began, at the entrance to the *kipuka*. Beside the trail at this point, mingled with the endemic Hawaiian plants, are several interesting foreigners, such as an avocado tree whose weighty seed can only have been left there by some picnicker years ago. At the *kipuka*'s 4,000-foot elevation the avocado is far above its optimum range, yet it thrives. Indeed, all plants thrive in the *kipuka*, whose soil is made not of decomposed lava but of many layers of volcanic ash, rich in nitrates and other nutrients. In one place this hos-

THE SACRED OHELO

A MAJESTIC KOA

THE IMMIGRANT PUKAMOLE

PUKIAWE: A RITUAL FUMIGANT

pitable soil nourishes a bed of enormous nasturtiums, two or three times the size of garden nasturtiums. Near by flourishes a colourful *puka-mole*, which has somehow found its way there from Peru.

Near the exit from the *kipuka* I noticed a low shrub with small stiff leaves, some of them with red or white berries: this is a native plant called the *pukiawe*. The Hawaiians found the berries unappetizing but sometimes threaded them into *lei*. The notion that *lei* are always made of flowers is relatively recent; in earlier times they were often made of berries, feathers or nuts.

Another use of the *pukiawe* was an odd ritualistic one. The Hawaiian world was hedged about with taboos; if, for example, a commoner allowed his shadow to fall on a chief, the penalty was death. The chiefs found this a trifle inconvenient when they wished to attend a feast without killing their people. A temporary dispensation, however, was possible: a chief smoked himself in the fumes of burning *pukiawe* branches to remove his lethal taboo long enough for a public frolic.

Emerging from the cool *kipuka*, I glanced to the west at the quiet peak volcano of Mauna Loa. Its low gentle curve stretched for miles along the horizon. No trace of smoke or steam was visible at its summit. It seemed sunk in slumber from which it would never awaken. Yet common sense and the record of the past insist that it will indeed awaken, and that this green island on its flank will someday sink in a sea of fire.

THE EDGE OF THE KIPUKA–MAUNA LOA IN BACKGROUND

3/ The Magic of Maui

We lived and breathed in cloudland . . . . Forests laced with frost; silvery, silent seas; shores of agate and of pearl; blue shadowy caverns; mountains of light, dissolving and rising again.   CHARLES WARREN STODDARD/ *SOUTH-SEA IDYLS*

The names of most of the major Hawaiian islands are so ancient that no interpretation of them is possible. To be sure, the names once had specific meanings, in times lost beyond all memory. However, one island—the nearest to the main island of Hawaii—has a name that is readily understood: it is called Maui after a famous demigod. Now, Maui was not born on the island that bears his name. He has been well known for countless years throughout Polynesia, the vast ocean expanse extending northward from New Zealand through the Society Islands and the Marquesas, and no one can say where he came from. But it is only to this island in the Hawaiian chain that Maui's name is attached.

To the ancient Hawaiians, Maui was not one of the great gods in the Polynesian pantheon: Lono, god of harvest and peace; Kane, father of living creatures; Ku, god of war; or Kaneloa, ruler of the world of ghosts. Maui was a youthful player of tricks, innocent ones as a rule. He was quick-witted, a benefactor of humanity, and he was mortal himself—he was killed while trying to steal the secret of eternal life from a goddess called The Guardian of the Night, so that he could give it to mankind.

Maui had several brothers, less smart than he, whom he could often bamboozle into doing his bidding. Once he went fishing with a magical line and hook, and while his brothers dutifully paddled the canoe Maui sat in the stern and caught something enormous far below the surface. As the brothers struggled to move the canoe forward to pull up the heavy catch, Maui warned them not to look backwards. He had hooked a small continent lying on the bottom of the sea and he feared that it might break in pieces if his brothers paused to stare at it before he had it safely moored. Unfortunately they did not heed him; they turned around to look and the continent did indeed come apart, separating into the eight Hawaiian Islands.

Maui could not only pull islands from the depths. When the sky fell down, pressing so close to the earth that the trees were bent over and men had to crawl about on their knees, Maui summoned the strength to push it back up. Today clouds occasionally come close to the earth again but they do not stay long for fear that Maui will return and shove them so far into the heavens that they will never find their way back. People who doubt the story need only glance at the trees for proof. The trunks, branches and twigs, being resilient, have regained their normal shape but the leaves are still pressed flat.

Many of the tales of Maui are ancient but a few are even more recent than the arrival of the Polynesians in Hawaii, perhaps only a thousand years ago. On the island that bears Maui's name there is a great mountain called Haleakala—The House of the Sun. It could as well be called The Prison of the Sun because of Maui. When he lived on the island with his mother and brothers, the length of the days was only three or four hours. The sun was fond of sleeping, so it raced across the sky in order to get back into bed as quickly as possible. Because of the short days Maui's mother did not have time to make her *tapa* cloth from the bark of the mulberry or the *mamaki* tree. By nightfall the *tapa* was still soggy and not sun-dried as it ought to have been.

Studying the situation, Maui observed that the sun rose in the morning by thrusting first one long leg—or beam—above the rim of Haleakala, and then another and another. The sun had 16 such legs spaced evenly around its circumference, on which it strode through heaven. Maui therefore secured 16 long ropes that he made into lassos, and in the darkness before dawn he hid in a crevice high up near the top of the mountain. When the first of the sun's legs appeared Maui threw a rope around it and tied it to a *wiliwili* tree; and so he did with the second, third and all the others until the sun was hopelessly caught.

At first Maui announced that he was going to kill the sun with an axe he had brought with him for the purpose, but when the sun craftily pointed out that *tapa* cloth would *never* dry in total darkness, a bargain was struck. The sun agreed to walk slowly across the sky, while Maui agreed to cut the ropes and release his prisoner.

It was probably not Maui's benefactions to man that caused the Hawaiians to name the island after him. More likely it was because there was a magical charm about the demigod that the Hawaiians found somehow reflected in the beautiful, haunting land. Visitors, and even permanent residents on other islands who are able to set aside their local pride, tend to agree that there is a special air about Maui —or at any rate about east Maui—a bewitching place where a man can see strange things and believe he sees things even stranger. A good many years ago, in 1909, as staid an organization as the U.S. Bureau of American Ethnology published a book called *Unwritten Literature of Hawaii.* In it is this passage: "Of what nature were the gods of the old times, and how did the ancient Hawaiians conceive of them? As of beings having the form, the powers, and the passions of humanity, yet standing above and somewhat apart from men. One sees, as through a mist, darkly, a figure, standing, moving; in shape a plant, a tree or vine-clad stump, a bird, a taloned monster, a rock carved by the fire-queen, a human form, a puff of vapour—and now it has given place to vacancy. ... Or again, a traveller meets a creature of divine beauty, all smiles and loveliness. The infatuated mortal, smitten with hopeless passion, offers blandishments; he finds himself by the roadside, embracing a rock." The vision and the roadside would be, surely, in east Maui.

Haleakala is a national park. A well-engineered road, full of switchbacks, leads to the summit of the 10,000-foot mountain where Maui caught the sun. From the summit one can look down to the southwest and see, across a narrow channel, the low-lying island of Kahoolawe. It is one of the two islands in the archipelago that are almost never visited. The other is Niihau, which is owned in its entirety (72 square miles) by a family named Robinson whose members operate a cattle ranch there. The Robinsons have long been fanatical in their refusal to admit visitors, on the ground that they wish to preserve the bloodlines, language and customs of the 250 or so Hawaiians who live on the island and work for them.

Kahoolawe is a different case and deserves mention in a book about wilderness for a gloomy reason: it is a *man-made* wilderness. The island is on the lee side of Maui and thus is screened from rainfall, receiving only about 20 inches a year. Nonetheless Kahoolawe, within the memory of living Hawaiians, was green with drought-resistant grass and trees. But in the 1920s and 1930s it was overgrazed by herds of sheep and cattle, and after it could no longer support these animals it was turned into a bomb target for the military. Today it is a barren expanse of red dusty clay littered with shell casings, shrapnel and the black pellet droppings of seemingly immortal goats.

The sad little island of Kahoolawe is worth only a glance from the summit of Haleakala. The real spectacle lies down past a man's boots, where he can see spread out below him a huge crater 3,000 feet deep, eight miles long and three wide. The whole inner top of the mountain is missing. The great depression is commonly called Haleakala Crater, to the annoyance of geologists who keep pointing out that it was only partially caused by volcanism. Most of it was excavated by stream erosion in ancient times when the pattern of wind and rainfall must have been quite different from today's. The streams cut two large gaps through the wall of the then-dormant volcano—Koolau at the head of Keanae Valley to the northwest, and Kaupo to the southeast. After this occurred Haleakala became active again and erupted several more times, sending flows of lava pouring out through the gaps and covering almost all the signs of erosion.

From the mountaintop a trail leads into the crater, across its long floor, out through Kaupo Gap and down to the sea, a hike of about 20 miles through one of the most strangely beautiful landscapes on earth. The trail, its upper reaches called Sliding Sands for a reason that soon becomes clear to anyone walking on it, descends a slope of reddish-brown ash and cinders. For the first 1,000 feet of descent no plants are visible among the scorched stones. In the clear still air at that high altitude the crunch of cinders underfoot seems uncommonly loud. Tiny puffs of dust arise and hang motionless. The division between areas of sunlight and shadow is very sharp. Below, scattered on the level crater floor, there are several symmetrical volcanic mounds and cones in shades of ochre and orange, black and grey. In the distance they seem small but as a man approaches them they turn out to be several hundred feet high. He half expects to see two globe-helmeted figures in suits of metallic cloth, wearing little American flags as shoulder patches, come hopping out from behind one of the cones and start setting up a package of instruments.

Growing on the sides of the cones are round moon-coloured plants, some of them as large as bushel baskets: Haleakala silverswords. The Hawaiians, who had no word for metal in their language before the coming of white men, called the plant *ahinahina*, or "grey-grey", a repetition that served to make the point for people who had never seen polished silver or burnished steel. The leaves of the silversword are long and narrow, incurving to the shape of a globe, and they derive their colour from a dense feltlike covering of fine hair.

All plants of course are adaptations or designs that are successful in their particular environments, but on close inspection the silversword seems to go beyond mere success to something close to a miracle. It is found only at elevations of 7,000 to 10,000 feet on Haleakala—although a few specimens may still be surviving at similar heights on the volcanic island of Hawaii—and only in conditions that would be quickly fatal to other plants. It is desert-dry within the crater; at night the temperature often falls below freezing while by day the sun is merciless. Yet the silversword survives to an age of as much as 20 years and then, having reached a diameter of about two feet, it suddenly produces a magnificent flower stalk perhaps six feet high on which nod hundreds of purplish blossoms. After this effort it dies.

As a protection from cold the growing point of the silversword is buried deep in its globe of incurved leaves. Against the drying sun and wind the plant presents the narrow leaves characteristic of most desert vegetation. But within the leaves, where other plants have countless microscopic air spaces, the silversword has a jelly-like substance that stores water. Outside, the tiny grey hairs both deflect wind and turn sunlight aside. In cross section, instead of being round or convex like most hairs, they are seen to be flat or concave. Thus they do not focus light on the leaves, like lenses, but reflect it.

It would seem that so well designed a plant would have little difficulty surviving, but a careful count in 1927 turned up barely 100 specimens remaining in Haleakala, where once there had been so many that the cinder cones seemed bathed in perpetual silvery moonlight. Mountain climbers destroyed some of them; as Europeans fasten sprigs of edelweiss on their hats to signify that they have climbed one alp or another, people who ascended Haleakala used to carry down small silverswords. Or they would uproot the largest ones and roll them like huge snowballs down the cones. At one time thousands of the plants were picked, dried and shipped to the Orient as ornaments. Goats, however, did even more damage than men, devouring the seedlings as fast as they sprouted. The species was saved at almost its final moment by the National Park Service, which planted some specimens and fenced them off; they then began a programme to wipe out the goats, deputizing hunters as rangers so they could shoot the animals on park land. (Many Hawaiians are fond of the meat. A prime goat is worth as much as £10

The silversword, named for the silvery hairs on its leaves, is one of the world's rarest plants, growing only in Haleakala Crater on the island of Maui. The plant takes as much as 15 years to produce its soaring six-foot bloom, after which it withers and dies.

on the market.) By 1973 the silversword, though still endangered and in need of every bit of protection it could get, had increased in number to about 2,000, and the goats, though still in the neighbourhood, had become skittish about venturing across the open floor of the crater to reach the plants on the cones.

Archaeologists have uncovered a good many stone platforms and terraces in and around Haleakala Crater, together with several ancient graves—it was the custom of Hawaiians to bury their dead, particularly people of prominence, in remote and inaccessible places. Near the midpoint of the crater there is a black hole about 10 feet in diameter, rimmed with a jagged rampart of lava spatter, that was apparently thought by the Hawaiians to be a bottomless pit. (Today it is choked with rubble about 70 feet underground and appears to have been a vent for escaping gas in some long-ago eruption.) The Hawaiians used the pit to dispose of the umbilical cords of babies, which were wrapped in *tapa* cloth or, more recently, placed in bottles. It was believed that this would make the children strong and prevent them from becoming thieves, as might happen if the cords were casually discarded, then found and eaten by rats.

At the eastern end of the crater near Paliku Cabin, a park service rest hut, the trail turns south to descend the Kaupo Gap. At this point there is a notch like a rear gun sight high in the crater wall. On the other side of the wall, on the outer slope of Haleakala, lies the cloud-filled valley of Kipahulu. Trade winds constantly push clouds up the valley towards the notch in the high wall and often they spill through into the crater in a swirl of rain and mist. Thus for a few hundred yards around Paliku there is an area of vegetation unmatched anywhere else in Haleakala; the clouds, drifting deeper into the dry crater, quickly lose all their moisture and vanish in the brilliantly clear air.

The trail approaches Paliku across a field of broken, spiny blocks of lava crazily jumbled together. If clouds are coming down through the notch, the lava field is wrapped in thick mist with low, twisted bushes and trees materializing and disappearing in it. Their crooked, beckoning branches seem to be clutching at shreds and streamers of fog slowly gliding past. The idea inevitably strikes a man that Macbeth must have encountered the three witches in a place very much like this —an idea that loses nothing when a wild, forlorn, nonhuman cry comes curling through the mist from somewhere close at hand.

There may be, on a good day, several wild, forlorn, nonhuman cries,

Elusive and rarely photographed, the Hawaiian honeycreepers are the most colourful and diversified family of native songbirds in the islands. Of the 20-odd species of honeycreepers, four are shown at right in Kipahulu Valley on Maui. Each of the four has a bill suited to the bird's preferred diet. The iiwi's bill is long and curved, enabling it to dip deep inside tubular flowers to get at their nectar. The bills of the apapane, the amakihi and the akohekohe are shorter and only slightly curved; these species favour the nectar of more open flowers, as well as insects, for food—in the case of the akohekohe, caterpillars.

THE IIWI, ADULT (LEFT) AND JUVENILE

THE APAPANE

THE AMAKIHI

THE AKOHEKOHE

and after an instant's hesitation a listener is glad to hear them. They are the calls of the Hawaiian goose, the *nene* (pronounced *nay-nay*), which is being bred in captivity and set free to establish itself in the wild at Paliku. *Nene*, which are believed to have evolved from Canada goose stock, are the state birds of Hawaii, and had been so cut down by hunters, predators and disease that in the late 1940s there were probably fewer than 50 of them left in the world. Since then federal and state propagation projects have increased their number to more than 1,000, some of them reared by the Severn Wildfowl Trust in England and air-freighted halfway around the globe for release on Maui. They often remain near the release site for some time, feeding on the cloud-watered grass and shiny black *kukaenene* berries there.

Nene bear a superficial resemblance to Canada geese, though their necks appear silvery instead of black. Their natural habitat is brushy upland between 5,000 and 7,000 feet, both on Maui and the island of Hawaii, and they are a great curiosity among waterfowl in that they forsook the water thousands of years ago. They rarely swim, except in a clumsy way in captivity, and in the process of evolution they have lost half the webbing on their feet.

When clouds lift away from the cliff above Paliku, a prominent rock called Pohaku Palaha becomes visible up there. It is the central reference point of bygone times, the surveyor's mark from which royal land grants were measured. Hawaiian kings had a remarkably equitable, sensible method of distributing real estate, at least among the chiefs, or *alii*, as they were called. Land grants were made in great triangles, with their apexes on mountaintops and their broad bases extending out into the ocean far below. The logic was that the necessities of life are to be found at various altitudes: each man needs hardwood for weapons and tools, *koa* trees for canoes, land for dry farming, land for wet farming, birds for eating and birds for ornament, a share of the sea for fishing and for recreation, and so on, all of which can be found only in triangular plots radiating down from pinnacles.

The trail leading out through Kaupo Gap goes down about 6,000 feet in eight miles to the sea, a pleasant slope easily descended. The vegetation grows thicker along the way; in its midst there are a good many large shrubs or small trees with leathery, dark green leaves and, in summer, clusters of brick-red flowers. These are sandalwoods, of which about eight species are found in Hawaii, where the tree has had a melancholy history. Sandalwood was—and still is—highly prized in the Orient, where its close-grained heartwood is used in ornamental carving and cabinetwork. It is richly scented, and is burned both for incense and as an insect repellent. When white men discovered that sandalwood was abundant in Hawaii a hectic and almost maniacal trade sprang up in it. In exchange for money or goods, mostly the latter, local chiefs traded great quantities of sandalwood at prices that ranged upward from £50 a ton, an important sum in the period (1815-1830) when the traffic was at its height. The actual collection was done, of course, by the common people, who were forced to go up into the mountains to cut trees and carry down the logs. If a chief wished to buy a shipyard-built schooner or other small ship, his subjects were ordered to dig a large pit that had the dimensions and shape of the proposed vessel and to fill the pit with closely packed sandalwood. This was considered a fair swap by white traders, who then transported the wood to China and received silks, porcelain and other goods worth 10 times as much as the ship. Hawaiian chiefs drove their subjects so hard to collect wood that there was little time for anything else, even farming, with the result that the islands were seriously threatened by famine. However, by about 1830 all the marketable sandalwoods had been cut down and the trade ended. Hawaiian workers, who were not only strong-backed but smart, also surreptitiously destroyed as many sandalwood seedlings as they could find so that they would not have to return in later years to harvest the trees. Today the sandalwoods have made a fair comeback, but it will be another century or two before truly large ones are again common.

As the trail from Kaupo Gap approaches the sea, the white waves breaking along the coast come increasingly into focus. With binoculars a man can look out into the Alenuihaha Channel, which separates east Maui from the island of Hawaii, and see—particularly in the months from November to May—humpback whales frolicking there with their calves. Considerable numbers of these creatures, which weigh as much as 60 tons, congregate in Hawaiian waters to breed. Humpbacks are black with white undersides, although occasionally a pure white one appears. Moby Dick was a sperm whale, not a humpback, but the sight is enough to bemuse any reader of Herman Melville.

The green coast and the constantly changing blue of the sea, the coconut palms nodding by the shore in the steady, gentle breeze of the trades, can hold a man transfixed for hours. He can, with Mark Twain, "sun himself all day long under the palm trees, and be no more troubled by his conscience than a butterfly would". But the long downhill

trail ends at a coastal road and sooner or later the road must be followed. Several miles to the east lie the entrances—or, at any rate, the access points—of two wild valleys, beyond the utmost capability of jeeps, requiring an uphill scramble on foot. The valleys are Kipahulu, from whose upper end the clouds glide down through the notch into Haleakala Crater, and Waihoi.

In the summer of 1972 photographer Dan Budnik climbed into Waihoi and emerged with the pictures on pages 98 to 105. Kipahulu was explored in 1967 by a group of scientists sponsored by The Nature Conservancy. Theirs was the first study of the whole ecology of the valley and to this day it remains unsurpassed, although nonscientists will find parts of it a good deal more fascinating than others. Botanically, Kipahulu proved to be the greatest stronghold of endemic plants in all of Hawaii. Only 10 per cent of those found there have been introduced to the islands by man; all the rest, some 200 species including at least 15 previously unknown, are endemic, or indigenous. One of the expedition's botanists, Dr. Charles Lamoureux of the University of Hawaii, was so impressed that he concluded—in language a good deal more exuberant than scientists generally use—that "Kipahulu . . . offers an opportunity [for study] not available elsewhere on this planet".

The birds of Kipahulu, some of which are pictured on page 87, are perhaps of more interest to laymen. Indeed, one species that had been thought to be extinct since the 19th Century was found to be living in the valley. However, the names of Hawaiian birds have so odd an appearance in print, and their extinction or near-extinction has been so puzzling, that some preliminary explanation seems worthwhile.

A written language for Hawaiians was devised in the 19th Century by missionaries, who tried to express the rich, spoken language with an alphabet of only 12 letters—the five vowels plus the consonants h, k, l, m, n, p and w. Because there are so few letters it is necessary to make the most of them; a man cannot go far wrong if he pronounces every letter he possibly can. Thus the bird called the *ou* is pronounced *oh-oo*; the *o-o* is *oh-oh*, and so on. To some non-Hawaiians the names may *look* silly, but in fact they are musical and in some cases onomatopoeic —to some, *elepaio* suggests the call of the bird itself. As one Hawaiian ornithologist has observed, not without annoyance, "People on the mainland would be a lot more concerned with our endangered species if only they were named the Red, White and Blue Warbler or the American Golden Owl. As it is, our only endemic owl is the *pueo*."

Waterfalls wide and narrow, powered by 200 inches of rain a year, feed the Palikea Stream and its tributaries in Maui's Kipahulu Valley.

Now to the loss of Hawaii's birds. When the islands were discovered by white men there were 69 species found nowhere else in the world. Twenty-five of them are now known or believed to be extinct and another 27 are considered rare or endangered. How this depletion should have come about was for many years a mystery.

Explanations that at first seemed obvious and conclusive turned out on thoughtful examination to be only partially true or not true at all. Only two things were certain: first, that for a century after the arrival of Captain Cook competent observers on all the islands had seen Hawaii's endemic birds ranging in goodly numbers from the beaches to the high mountain forests; and second, that by the end of the 19th Century the birds were fast disappearing or had already vanished. It seemed likely that one cause was the destruction of part of their habitat, taken over by huge plantations and ranches; another was that their food plants had been devoured by cattle and goats or crowded out by rampaging imported vegetation. Still another probable factor was the introduction of continental predators such as house cats, which ran wild, and the small Indian mongoose, *Herpestes auropunctatus*, which was brought to Hawaii in 1883 to prey on rats in the sugar-cane fields. (Although mongooses do destroy rodents, they also destroy ground-nesting birds and have been known to kill animals many times larger than themselves. Full-grown mongooses weigh only a couple of pounds but can fell fawns and even donkeys by attacking them around the mouth and throat.) But these factors did not provide the whole answer. Something strange and unaccountable was also taking place.

In 1902 the ornithologist H. W. Henshaw wrote in bafflement: "The author has lived in Hawaii only six years, but within this time large areas of forest, which are yet scarcely touched by the axe save on the edges and except for a few trails, have become almost absolute solitude. One may spend hours in them and not hear the note of a single native bird. Yet a few years ago these areas were abundantly supplied with native birds. . . . The ohia blossoms as freely as it used to and secretes abundant nectar for the Iiwi, Apapane and Amakihi. The ieie still fruits, and offers its crimson spike of seeds, as of old, to the Ou. So far as the human eye can see, their old home offers to the birds practically all that it used to, but the birds themselves are no longer there. . . . The abandonment of forest tracts under such circumstances seems inexplicable, and the writer can recall no similar phenomenon among American birds."

The native birds did not vanish on all the islands simultaneously

—on Lanai, for example, they flourished until 1923, when a sudden decline began. And on one of the remote Leeward Islands the Laysan finch is probably as numerous today as it ever was. Further, extinction and survival are related to altitude—in lowland areas the endemic honeycreepers have disappeared, yet remnant populations still exist in upland forest areas like the Kipahulu Valley, above 3,000 feet, and in the Alakai Swamp on the island of Kauai, at 4,200 feet.

The elements of the mystery were pieced together and published in 1968 in a brilliant scientific paper by Dr. Richard E. Warner, who had spent several years studying Hawaiian birds. It was plain enough that the major factor in their disappearance was disease; encroachment on their habitat, reduction of food supply and increase of predators were important but secondary. But what were the diseases and how had they been spread?

Just as the Hawaiian people had never developed resistance to influenza or measles, Hawaiian birds had no resistance to avian malaria, which is common among mainland birds and is caused by a microscopic parasite in their blood. Hawaiian birds were also highly vulnerable to bird pox, or bumblefoot, a tumour-producing disease of domestic poultry. In Warner's view, the potential for avian malaria had probably existed in Hawaii for thousands of years. Migratory shore birds and ducks, coming to the islands from the mainland, undoubtedly carried the blood parasite—but for some reason it was not transmitted to the native birds. Caged pet birds and foreign birds introduced by the early colonists might also have caused the disaster. Bird pox was a different matter; it had come to Hawaii with the barnyard fowl of white men. Still, how it had been passed from chickens to wild forest birds remained a puzzle.

The answer, Warner found, lay in an incident that had occurred in the port of Lahaina on Maui in 1826. In that year the ship *Wellington*, having last filled her water casks at San Blas on the west coast of Mexico, put in at Lahaina to fill them again. The sailors assigned to this duty dumped the dregs from the casks into a pure stream, not noticing or more likely not caring that the dregs were alive with small wriggling larvae. In that manner the mosquito, which had failed to reach Hawaii in 20 million years, arrived at last. The particular mosquito was *Culex pipiens fatigans*, which inhabits tropical and subtropical regions. It is now found on the main Hawaiian islands from sea level to elevations of about 3,000 feet.

Culex was the carrier that transmitted blood parasites and viruses from migratory birds and domestic poultry to Hawaii's endemic birds. As *Culex* made its way from island to island the forests one after another fell silent. Even at altitudes above 3,000 feet, where the mosquitoes are not found in significant numbers, the silence spread. The insects did not go up to the birds; the birds came down to the insects. It had been the long-established habit of Hawaiian birds to migrate, during the season of winter storms, from the high country to the lowlands—and when they descended into territory occupied by *Culex* they were bitten and mortally infected.

In some conclusive experiments Dr. Warner captured small numbers of Laysan finches on their tiny home island, 900 miles from Honolulu, where the mosquito had never become established. The birds were taken to Honolulu in a cage shrouded in several layers of cheesecloth, and for two months they thrived in it. But when the cheesecloth was removed and mosquitoes were allowed to enter the cage, all of the finches developed bird pox and perished. In a similar test on the island of Kauai, other Laysan finches prospered in cages but died of avian malaria soon after the screening was removed. Later Dr. Warner captured a few individuals of other endemic species—*apapane, amakihi* and lesser *amakihi*—at an elevation of about 4,000 feet on Kauai and took them down to the lowlands, where they too developed malaria and died.

Today it is only in the highlands that Hawaii's rare endemic birds are found. Warner thinks they may be developing disease-resistant forms and hopes they may someday be able to return to the pestilent lowlands. However, this is at best only a hope, and some powerful factors are arrayed against it. In recent years, introduced game birds such as pheasants and wild turkeys have been found to carry, among other diseases, avian encephalomyelitis and botulism. It is impossible to say what resistance to these diseases the endemic birds may have, although very likely they have none. And in California there exists a mosquito called *Culex pipiens pipiens*, a cousin of the insect already established in Hawaii, that can thrive in higher altitudes. If *pipiens* establishes itself in the islands, having reached them not in a water cask but in the cabin of a jet plane, the last of the rare birds may be doomed.

It was Dr. Warner who led The Nature Conservancy's expedition of scientists into Maui's Kipahulu Valley, which slopes gradually upwards until at 7,300 feet it ends at the wall that separates it from the crater of Haleakala. As they ascended from the lower elevations to 2,500 feet

Ohia trees thrust their limbs through the Kipahulu Valley cloud forest, where constant moisture helps them grow 50 to 100 feet tall.

they found exactly what Warner had expected—dense populations of *Culex* and not a single bird belonging to Hawaii's remarkable honeycreeper family. But by about 3,000 feet the mosquitoes disappeared and the honeycreepers began to be seen in increasing numbers, among them *apapane, iiwi, amakihi* and Maui creepers. Only the latter is considered a rare and endangered species but the relative abundance of the other birds seemed an encouraging sign, suggesting that in the upper reaches of Kipahulu—where in all the years since Cook's arrival in 1778 only a handful of white men have ever ventured—there might be something very surprising.

Among the scientists there were four who had special competence in ornithology: Warner; Dr. Andrew Berger of the University of Hawaii; Winston Banko, a research biologist in the Bureau of Sport Fisheries and Wildlife of the U.S. Department of the Interior; and Gerald Swedberg of the Hawaii State Division of Fish and Game. It is worth stressing the competence of the men—when amateurs report the sighting of unusual birds doubts can be raised, but in this case there are none. All four men saw the *akohekohe*, or crested honeycreeper, described by the Hawaiian Audubon Society as "possibly the rarest of the living native Hawaiian mountain birds", not once but several times each. Some of the birds were feeding on the crimson blossoms of an *ohia* tree almost directly above a campsite at 6,000 feet.

It fell to Winston Banko to make the two most startling discoveries of the expedition. Binoculars in hand, Banko was walking alone on a trail at about 5,800 feet when he saw "a small, dull, yellowish bird with a dark eye stripe and a moderately long, distinctly sickle-shaped bill". He held his binoculars on it for nearly half a minute at fairly close range but was unable to recognize it. However, he did have time to make note of every field mark that might be useful in identification, noting in particular the downcurving bill with an upper segment more than twice the length of the lower.

Half an hour later Banko saw a second such bird at a slightly lower elevation, and still later he spotted a third. He made a leisurely examination of it with his glasses at a distance of only 25 feet, so close that he could pick out every feather, but still he could not identify it. "The problem," he says with a wry smile, "is that I had studied all the *living* birds of Hawaii, but not having studied the extinct ones, I wasn't prepared for what I was looking at. As soon as I got back to camp I grabbed a reference book and there, among the old photographs, it was." The birds he had rediscovered were Maui *nukupuu*, believed by almost all ornithologists to have vanished many years ago. The last sighting had been in 1896.

Banko was also fortunate enough to have a long close-up view of another exceptionally rare honeycreeper, the Maui parrotbill, that had been seen only once before in the 20th Century, in 1950. "I had been looking particularly for the parrotbill," he says, "and suspected it might be found—if at all—high up in the valley. I saw it at nearly 6,500 feet —and of course, there's no mistaking a bird like that." In its particular adaptation the parrotbill has developed by far the most formidable beak of all the honeycreepers, enabling it to tear the bark from trees or crush twigs to get at insect larvae inside.

The discovery of the rare birds has been, not only for Banko and Warner but also for every naturalist in Hawaii, a source of delight and fear. Without exception they feel that Kipahulu Valley, which through the efforts of The Nature Conservancy was added to Haleakala National Park in 1969, must be kept closed indefinitely to everyone but qualified researchers who can demonstrate a genuine need for going there. "The preservation of this area intact," Banko says, "is of paramount—absolute—importance." But it is no easy proposition, politically, to exclude the taxpayers from land the taxpayers own. "Prayer may help."

It may indeed. It may also be helpful if men develop the sort of love for Maui, the unwillingness to inflict even the slightest injury, that filled Mark Twain when he saw Hawaii and that remained with him for the rest of his life:

"No alien land in all the world has any deep strong charm for me but that one, no other land could so longingly and so beseechingly haunt me, sleeping and waking, through half a lifetime, as that one has done. Other things leave me, but it abides; other things change, but it remains the same. For me its balmy airs are always blowing, its summer seas flashing in the sun; the pulsing of its surfbeat is in my ear; I can see its garlanded crags, its leaping cascades, its plumy palms drowsing by the shore, its remote summits floating like islands above the cloud rack; I can feel the spirit of its woodland solitudes, I can hear the splash of its brooks; in my nostrils still lives the breath of flowers that perished twenty years ago."

The Remaking of a Valley

PHOTOGRAPHS BY DAN BUDNIK

Lying just inland from the east coast of the island of Maui the secluded three-and-a-half-square-mile Waihoi Valley imparts an almost palpable air of mystery. Its very look is strange. Carved out of the lower flank of the Haleakala Crater and bounded by near-vertical cliffs, the valley rises from a floor rather like a broad, tilted plate, gently sloping up to about 3,600 feet, then sharply climbing in ridges to the rim of the crater at almost 7,000 feet.

The main mystery of Waihoi, however, is not geological but botanical. Unlike other valleys on Maui, particularly Kipahulu to the southwest, Waihoi has no stands of giant trees and little diversity of plant life. The birds that abound in the forests of Kipahulu find no haven in Waihoi and seldom appear there.

Trying to explain the reasons for this lack of luxuriance, botanists theorize that at some point in the past something interfered with the valley's primeval growth. The nature of the disturbance is unknown. It may have been a volcanic eruption, even though no recent lava flows are visible. The cause may have been landslides, animals rooting for food, ancient Hawaiians planting taro, or a combination of these factors.

Whatever the agent, it interrupted the growth of the plants that, left undisturbed, might have made Waihoi as lush a place as Kipahulu, where some trees reach 100 feet in height.

But now there are signs that Waihoi is staging a comeback, spontaneously reforesting itself (opposite). A thick matting of three-foot-high false staghorn fern covers the valley's floor and lower slopes and lines its shallow streams. This pioneer plant grows not only in the Hawaiian Islands but in several other tropical and subtropical areas as well. In Waihoi, however, a number of plants endemic to the islands— growing nowhere else—have begun to re-establish themselves. *Ohia* and *olapa* trees, *naupaka*, broussaisias and others poke uncertainly through the ferns here and there on the lower slopes, increasing in number, fullness and stature on the ridges.

The growth is slow; the soil on which the staghorn ferns and endemic plants have gained a hold is thin and nutrient-poor. Men now living cannot expect to see the ultimate outcome, but it may be that, given no further disturbance, the increasingly sturdy endemic plants will eventually crowd out the ferns and give a new luxuriance to Waihoi.

False staghorn ferns fringe a rocky stream in a southern corner of the Waihoi Valley. This species of fern is a pioneer plant—one of the first to recolonize a disrupted area; currently the most abundant plant in the lower valley, it may in time be crowded by the scrubby ohia trees seen growing sparsely among the ferns. The cloud-shrouded ridge in the background separates the Waihoi from its much lusher neighbour, the Kipahulu Valley.

Inundating the area, false staghorn fern covers the Waihoi Valley, unchallenged by other plants until it reaches the base of the ridge.

An Aggressive Pioneer

The first plant to reclaim the floor of Waihoi Valley, and its principal cover up to an altitude of about 3,600 feet, is the false staghorn fern. It is called staghorn probably because of its forking leaves, which look much like the antlers of a stag, and it is called false to distinguish it from the true staghorn, another Pacific fern to which it bears a little resemblance but no kinship whatever. The Hawaiians call it *uluhe*. In the old days they used its sturdy tangled branches for thatching their houses, and the juices of the plant for a laxative.

In the meagre soil of the lower part of the valley the false staghorn is the only plant that grows in any abundance. Below ground it advances by putting out rootstocks; above ground it forms a dense tangle of wiry fronds that range from a few inches to a few feet in length. No matter how matted false staghorns become as they grow, they are recognizable from a distance by their yellowish-green colour.

Nevertheless, this seemingly indomitable fern should eventually be driven out. For in flourishing it fortifies and enriches the soil with its roots and nutrients, thus preparing the way for other plant life to follow. *Ohia* and *olapa*, the most common trees throughout the Hawaiian Islands, will take root after them; in time the *ohia* and *olapa* will put up a forest cover, displace the false staghorn and encourage the colonization of a diversity of other plants.

A clump of fern fronds shows the tangled growth that chokes out most other vegetation.

Flanked by ferns and yellow broussaisia flowers, a Cyanea aculeatiflora spreads its leaves over the delicate white bloom at its base.

A Flourishing Forest on the Heights

One of the enigmas of the Waihoi Valley is evidence that whatever upheaval disturbed the valley floor apparently did not reach its ridges. Here a number of endemic plants compete with the staghorn fern for living space. In the lower altitudes they are sparse in number and small in stature; but above 4,000 feet they multiply and thicken. They finally surpass the fern along the tops of the ridges, flowering into a fully-fledged forest that spills over into the canyons of adjoining Kipahulu Valley.

None of the plants in this forest grow anywhere but in the Hawaiian Islands; some, like the *Cyanea aculeatiflora* (*left*), are endemic to the east coast of Maui. The graceful, broad-leaved cyanea belongs to the lobelia family, species of which occur elsewhere in the islands and other parts of the world. But through long isolation on Maui the *Cyanea aculeatiflora* has evolved prickly flowers lacking in other lobelias.

The antiquity of the cyanea and of the other flowers of the Waihoi forest (*right and overleaf*) has given many of them a place in Hawaiian folklore. One legend about the *naupaka* attributes its peculiar form—as if it were minus one petal (*overleaf, lower left*)—to a lovers' quarrel. The piqued maiden is said to have torn apart a *naupaka* flower and told her lover that if he wanted her back he must find her a perfect bloom. He could find only the odd-shaped *naupaka* and died of a broken heart.

Seen in detail, the blossom of the Cyanea aculeatiflora reveals the prickles that distinguish the plant from lobelias elsewhere in the world.

A labordia, a member of the poisonous strychnine family, flaunts its vivid yellow-orange flower against a backdrop of glossy green leaves.

Small yellow blossoms mark the Broussaisia arguta, a relative of the hydrangea.

The Nothocestrum longifolium, called the aiea by the Hawaiians, is related to the tomato, the potato and tobacco. Its seeds are dispersed by birds that dote on its orange-red fruit.

A naupaka (below), looking as though it were missing one of its petals, grows on a Waihoi Valley ridge. It is one of the relatively few Hawaiian plants that are in flower all year round.

A Trematolobelia macrostachys, a species of lobelia, leans over the south ridge, extending its nectar-filled blossoms out over the valley.

4/ Refuge on a Reef

Against the illimitable blue of the sky, over the unfathomable blue of the ocean the sea birds of the Pacific wing the cycle of their lives. For them the ocean is a larder: the islands and atolls their mating ground and nurseries. GEORGE C. MUNRO/ *BIRDS OF HAWAII*

Before dawn the sky over the Pacific was like a sheet of dark blue glass. From below the eastern horizon, light and heat began to play on it. The stars squeezed shut and the sky expanded, growing pale and taut. Suddenly the sky shattered, falling in countless tinkling fragments, while overhead, replacing the stars, white birds soared.

The island is small, a sand-covered coral platform only about half a mile long and a few hundred yards wide. There are no trees on it, only broad patches of tough narrow-leaved grass and mats of yellow-flowered puncture vine. Along one side of the island runs a beach of coral sand; on the other there are limestone reefs and shelves. During the night a half-dozen green sea turtles, big as overturned wheelbar-rows, have hauled themselves up on the beach to sleep. Not far away two brown-grey seals, each with her single black-velvet pup, are doz-ing on the sand. In the shallow water near them the silhouette of a little wave, less than a foot high, suddenly turns solid and moves against the grain of the other waves—a shark's fin.

The island is very low. The highest point on it is only 12 feet above the level of the sea. From there one can see about seven miles to the ho-rizon where in all directions there is no smoke, no sail, no ship, nothing. The island is far from any travelled sea lanes; almost no one ever goes there intentionally. The discoverers of it surely went there by mistake.

In 1822 two English whaleships, the *Pearl* and the *Hermes*, cruising in consort, ran into the coral reef and broke up. The survivors built a 30-ton craft out of the wreckage, the *Deliverance*, and navigated it 1,100 miles southeast to Honolulu. Today the charts show this coral bank as Pearl and Hermes Reef:

Pearl and Hermes Reef is in fact an atoll, a half-submerged coral ring about 15 miles wide enclosing a very pale green lagoon in the dark blue sea. There are a few tiny islands along the rim of the lagoon but this one, Southeast Island, is the largest and of greatest consequence. The rest are big sand bars. The atoll marks the place where once there existed a high volcanic island, perhaps as large as Oahu. Now it is worn down by rain, wind and waves so that no trace of it is visible, although if a drill bit were sunk through the sand and coral it would strike black lava roots a few hundred feet down.

In the early-morning light two structures appear on the island. One is a flimsy tower of metal posts and angle irons with something white lashed to its top: a five-gallon metal water can completely covered with sea-bird droppings. It might serve to alert a navigator approaching the low island. The other is a redwood sign. Carved on it in large half-inch-deep letters is "Hawaiian Islands National Wildlife Refuge/Pearl and Hermes Reef/Southeast Island". Below that there is "No Trespassing" in English and Japanese. Aside from the tower and the sign there are not many evidences of human life except for a temporary camp in which a few men are living.

The birds that had replaced the stars were white albatrosses and red-tailed tropic birds. At lower levels shearwaters, petrels, boobies and frigate birds dipped and soared. On the sand, in the grass and on the bare limestone rock there were white eggs and speckled eggs, oval eggs and conical eggs, eggs that weighed less than an ounce and others that weighed three-quarters of a pound. Chicks were everywhere. The newly hatched sooty terns were little grey fluffballs spotted with brown. The infant frigate birds were ugly enough to rouse religious thoughts in the mind of a heathen. Surely nothing could be *that* homely without being part of some grand design: stark naked, without even a visible hair or pinfeather; bright grey skin, the colour of a bookmaker's felt hat; covered with permanent large goose-pimples; potbellied, scrawny; mad-eyed and squirming with lust for food.

The young albatrosses, although they were already about six months old, two feet tall and had six-foot wingspreads, were still only chicks and not nearly as ferocious as they tried to appear. Some were just

learning to fly and would make 20- or 30-foot hops that often ended in ridiculous crashes that seemed to embarrass them a good deal. When a
man approached them they would snap their beaks rapidly with a sound
like castanets but then they would trip over their own feet and fall
down. Sometimes they made little peeping sounds. There were about
6,000 of them on the island, so that it was impossible to walk very far
without running into one. Perhaps 80 per cent of them were Laysan albatrosses, with white heads, breasts and underparts; the upper surfaces
of their wings and their tails are brownish black. The remaining birds
were black-footed albatrosses, first cousins of the Laysans, with black
bills and sooty brown heads and bodies. When they are standing on the
ground both birds, at least at first glance, suggest enormous sea gulls.
In the air, with their long, narrow wings outstretched in gliding flight,
they look like gliders. Their common name is gooney, or gooney
bird, a sailor's term that may derive from the old word "gawney", meaning a clownish fool. Still, although they have comical habits and often
get into ludicrous scrapes, they are—as birds go—fairly intelligent.

The air over the island was not, as might be expected in a rookery,
full of uproar and stench. The trade winds blew steadily from the northeast at about 10 miles an hour and the birds were fairly quiet except
when a man intruded directly among their eggs and chicks. At such
times they set up an incessant screaming, as they were doing now.
Walking in a blizzard of sooty terns so thick he could reach out and
catch them in midair in one hand was the man who has charge of the refuge, looking after the interests of the birds and the people of the United
States. Although he had arrived on the previous afternoon, a good deal
of time had been consumed in setting up camp; and now he was taking
his first careful look around. "Please," he said to the terns in a reasonable tone, "stop dropping guano on the administrator."

The name of the administrator is Eugene Kridler, pronounced with a
long "i", as in rider. He is a rugged man in his early fifties who works
for the Fish and Wildlife Service of the U.S. Department of the Interior. Two or three times a year he leaves his office on Oahu and journeys
out to the refuge to see what has been going on there. The refuge extends for more than 800 miles northwestward from the main Hawaiian
islands and comprises a chain of reefs, islets and atolls—Nihoa Island,
Necker Island, French Frigate Shoals, Gardner Pinnacles, Maro Reef,
Laysan Island, Lisianski Island and Pearl and Hermes Reef—that are
collectively one of the world's most important sea-bird nesting areas.

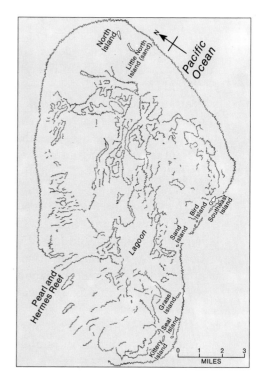

The classic semicircular shape of a
coral atoll appears on this map of Pearl
and Hermes Reef. Only 15 miles wide,
Pearl and Hermes covers more than
100,000 acres of reefs, islands and
lagoon within the barrier reef
(outermost line) separating it from the
ocean. The shorter lines mark coral
formations that are usually below
water; only the islands, which are
labelled, stand above the tide level.

The refuge also contains most of the Hawaiian monk seals still surviving on the planet, and is the last remaining nesting ground in the United States of the green sea turtle.

To reach the island, Kridler relies on the co-operation of the Coast Guard and the Navy, which sometimes have ships or helicopters operating in the neighbourhood and will take him along. In this instance a big Navy helicopter flying out of Midway Island had set him down on Pearl and Hermes with all his equipment, including aluminium bands for the birds, metal tags for the seal pups and turtles and an enormous slide calliper of the sort used by foresters to determine the diameter of trees. Kridler measures turtles with it.

The Navy had also provided him with a couple of burly assistants to help wrestle the turtles and the seals, which weigh as much as 300 and 700 pounds respectively. One of the assistants, a Chief Hospitalman named Marvin Cunningham, was an amateur naturalist who had accompanied Kridler on previous visits to the island. This time Cunningham hoped to find a seal, dead of natural causes, intact and not too fragrant, so that a skeleton could be secured for a museum. Museums are glad to have the skeletons of rare creatures so long as they are collected by people who know what they are about. Cunningham, whose main medical interest is in bacteriology, spent considerable time in Vietnam and sent back scores of carefully prepared rodent skins and skeletons to the Smithsonian Institution.

On this trip Cunningham was looking for Hawaiian monk seals, so called because the silhouette of their head and neck is thought to resemble that of a monk in a cowl; monk seals belong to an interesting branch of the pinnipeds, or fin-footed mammals. There are (or perhaps were) only three species, unusual among their kind in that they live in warm or subtropical waters. Several hundred of them still inhabit the Mediterranean, principally along the North African coast. At one time monk seals were numerous in the Caribbean, in the Bahamas and off the Florida coast, but they have probably all been slaughtered. The last sure sightings of them were made in 1949. Hawaiian monk seals were nearly wiped out as well, for their oil and skins, but have made a comeback since Theodore Roosevelt established the refuge in 1909. Kridler estimates their number today at about 1,000.

As Kridler made his morning reconnaissance he looked for signs that anyone had landed on the island since his last visit. "Do you know what could happen if there were a shipwreck out here?" he said.

It struck me that this would be a poor place for a man to be stranded.

"I wasn't thinking about *people*," he said. "What I worry about is rats. If a ship ploughs into one of these islands and the rats get ashore, they can wipe out a whole species before you know it. Ground-nesting birds are very vulnerable to rats." A few years ago a scientist from the Smithsonian, working in the outer islands, watched a rat attack an albatross on its nest. The albatross was so intent on brooding its egg that it defended itself only feebly and was killed.

Although it would be grim news if rats got ashore anywhere in the refuge, it would be disastrous on a couple of the islands because of the extreme rarity of the species living there. On Nihoa, and nowhere else on earth, live some greyish-brown millerbirds, so called because of their fondness for eating miller moths. When Kridler last estimated their number he put it at about 600. The island also is the only home of the Nihoa finch, a member of the Hawaiian honeycreeper family. In size and colour the birds resemble large canaries, with yellow heads and bodies, but they have powerful crushing beaks like those of miniature parrots. About 4,000 of them still survive. On Laysan in the highly saline interior lagoon there are some handsome little ducks, unique to that island, that have been fighting nip-and-tuck with extinction since 1923. In that year only seven of them existed; today there are probably about 175. The ducks, the finches and the millerbirds would vanish quickly if rats became established on their islands. In 1969 a Japanese fishing trawler ran aground at a speed of eight knots on Laysan. After the men were rescued they swore a great nine-jointed oath that rats had never set foot on *their* vessel, but when he inspected the wreck Kridler found several boxes of rat poison. "I had nightmares about it for some time," he said, "but either there really weren't any rats aboard or they failed to get ashore. That time, anyway."

There were no signs that strangers had been prowling on Pearl and Hermes in the immediate past, so Kridler turned his eye to legitimate visitors, the turtles on the beach. A full-grown green sea turtle is surprisingly powerful and when it is alarmed it moves like a bulldozer across the sand, heading straight for the water. To capture the turtles, which were asleep, Kridler and Cunningham sneaked up on them from the side and turned them over with sudden strong charges reminiscent of interior line play in football. They were careful to avoid the turtles' flippers, which are hard and bony on the front edges and can break a man's wrist with a solid blow. They also took heed of the turtles' mouths —green sea turtles do not snap aggressively, but may bite off a hand if it is carelessly offered to them. The two men turned over four big tur-

Scrawny and bare, a newborn frigate bird (above) hugs its nest in a clump of solanum shrub on Pearl and Hermes Reef, waiting to be fed small pieces of fish and squid that its parents steal from boobies. The adult female (right), gliding to the nest on its seven-foot wingspan, prepares to disgorge tidbits to its young as its mate looks on. Adults also eat tern chicks and turtle hatchlings when such delicacies are in season—mostly in summer.

tles with little trouble. A fifth one awakened, however, and began making for the water. Cunningham jumped in front of it and put his foot on its head, shoving it down hard into the sand. The turtle halted and in a moment Kridler hurried over and flipped it.

When green sea turtles are overturned they cannot right themselves again as can various other members of their kind, including snapping turtles. Upside down they can survive for weeks or months and were often carried in that manner for fresh food on long sailing voyages, to be butchered when needed. Kridler's turtles, as though they had some dim racial recollection of this, lay on their backs without struggling, occasionally uttering long, loud sighs. Two of them already had numbered metal tags attached to the trailing edges of their right front flippers, close to the body, where Kridler or his fellow workers had placed them in previous years. He took note of the numbers and then tagged the others, using pronged tags that are pinched shut with pliers. The turtles seemed not to notice, apparently being fairly insensitive to pain. One of them had been attacked by a shark that had bitten a semicircular piece out of the side of its shell about the size of half a dinner plate. The wound had healed in the manner of bark covering a gash on a tree.

Kridler took the dimensions of the turtle shells with his calliper, measuring length, width and thickness of body, which in a fair-sized creature came to 38.1, 29.2 and 13.7 inches. In weighing the turtles he and Cunningham slid them one at a time onto a piece of heavy canvas that had a slack loop of rope threaded through metal grommets around its edge. When the rope was pulled taut the canvas enclosed the turtle as in a hammock. The rope was then hooked onto a spring scale fastened to the middle of a stout eight-foot pole. They strained to lift the pole on their shoulders and when the hammock was clear of the ground I read the scale. The fair-sized creature weighed 295 pounds. Released, right side up, it rapidly heaved itself over the sand into the water and swam off at what seemed great speed, although it was probably only about 10 miles an hour.

"We're building up a file of information on the migration and growth rates of these turtles," Kridler said. "They're not an endangered species yet, but they soon may be. They're a great delicacy and bring high prices on the market. Right now we're co-operating with a scientist at the University of Hawaii who's trying to figure out if they can be raised commercially." So far Kridler has recaptured a number of turtles that have travelled from island to island within the refuge, and to some of the main inhabited Hawaiian islands—as much as 600 miles at times.

It was midsummer noon. Pearl and Hermes is not far from the intersection of the international date line and the Tropic of Cancer, and the sun there is like a sledge hammer. The water and the white, coarse coral sand reflected light and heat. The young albatrosses, facing into the wind, stood with wings outstretched, occasionally waving them to exercise and strengthen them. To cool off, the birds rocked back on their heels, lifting the soles of their triangular webbed feet so that the air could circulate under them. Networks of fine blood vessels enable their feet to serve as radiators, dissipating body heat. It is an effective mechanism except in one regard: unlike land birds, sea birds have no strong rear toes to support them when they rock back, and albatross chicks take some humiliating pratfalls before they get the hang of it.

Not all of the albatross eggs on the island had hatched. Some had been infertile and now, several months old, they were baking in the sun, full of green slime and gas. *Pow*! If a man picked up one of them, joggling it, there was a fair chance that it might explode in his hand. Sometimes an egg would burst spontaneously when no one was near. The sound was like a small light bulb breaking but the smell was thunderous, fortunately soon swept away by the breeze.

Scattered along the beach were scores of corked or capped glass bottles, seemingly a strange litter to be found in the far wilderness of the sea. Almost all of them were liquor or Japanese sake bottles tossed overboard from trawlers, merchantmen and passenger ships in many latitudes and carried to Pearl and Hermes by the wind and the ocean currents—the Kuroshio, the California and the Equatorial—that create a slow-moving clockwise flow of water in the North Pacific. A well-stoppered bottle will float for years or decades in the currents, and since there are literally millions of them adrift, even the most remote islands become strewn with them. In fact the remote islands, rarely reached by beachcombers and souvenir hunters, have many more bottles than the accessible ones. Among perhaps 200 bottles on Pearl and Hermes, two had messages or, at any rate, communications in them. One contained a tract from a West Coast Bible society announcing good news for sinners: the word of the Lord will reach them even at the ends of the earth. The other contained somewhat more earthly comfort: a photograph of a pretty Japanese girl, some Japanese cigarettes and matches.

Among the beached bottles were Japanese fishing floats, beautiful hand-blown glass globes of pale green, light blue and lavender that are used to hold nets upright in the water or to support lines of baited hooks. Many of them were the size of small grapefruit, others as large as basketballs and one, measured with Kridler's calliper, was nearly 16 inches in diameter. In use the floats are secured by light rope netting that sometimes breaks and sets them adrift. Occasionally in a storm a fishing boat may lose part or all of a tuna line, perhaps a mile long, with dozens of the big glass balls attached. They are eagerly sought by beach-combers in Hawaii, British Columbia, Washington and Oregon, who sell them to collectors and curio shops for as much as £20 apiece. There were at least 100 of various sizes on Pearl and Hermes, waiting for someone to pick them up.

In the heat of the afternoon Kridler took a census of some small birds commonly called Laysan finches. Canary-like, with heavy bills, they very much resemble Nihoa finches, and they too belong to the honeycreeper family. They are the only land birds on Pearl and Hermes and arrived as recently as 1967, when 50 pairs of them were transferred from their ancestral home on Laysan Island. They were in no immediate danger on Laysan, but it seemed a good idea to establish a colony of them on another island as insurance. To make an approximate count of the little birds, Kridler followed the wildlife biologist's standard procedure of sampling by transects, or swaths. At random in all parts of the island he selected 100 pieces of ground, each 100 feet long and $16\frac{1}{2}$ feet wide, and walked down the centre of each one, counting finches as he went. The population could be calculated by a ratio: the number of birds counted is to the total number of birds as the area of the 100 transects is to the total area of the island.

I set out to walk a few transects with Kridler. He began in the middle of the island, which was covered with wiry bunch grass in which the finches had built nests. On the ground between the bunches, terns were nesting too. Below the ground, in burrows they had dug in the soft earth, wedge-tailed shearwaters were nesting. Shearwaters are about 18 inches from bill to tail tip, grey brown above and whitish below, and can dig at a remarkable rate. It is very unsettling to walk across their nesting ground. Inevitably one steps on a concealed burrow, sinks to his knees in the earth and stands there horrified, not knowing if he has crushed an adult bird, a chick or an egg. Twice when I caved in their tunnels, adult shearwaters, hopping mad, dug their way out and scuttled and bounced away unhurt.

After 25 transects I left Kridler, found a patch of shade in the lee of a tent and sat watching him. Back and forth he went under the hammering sun, changing direction, counting his steps, counting birds, sinking into the earth and getting up, plodding across the hot sand and coral rock. Kridler believes in the old-fashioned virtues and regards himself as employed not by the bureaucracy in Washington but by his fellow citizens. On that small island, although it was 6,000 miles beyond eyeshot of civil-service headquarters on the Potomac, he seemed to have no thought of dogging the job by walking only 72 transects or even 99. He walked 100. He was dripping with sweat and limping when he came over to the tent and sat down to work out his ratio. The 50 pairs of finches had multiplied in five years and now, he figured, there were about 350 birds.

In the afternoon, isolated clouds drifted over the green lagoon, and the reflection of the sunlight from the water tinted the bottoms of the clouds. It was a good strong tint that must have been visible for many miles, if anyone beyond the horizon had been looking for it. Polynesian sailors, who were among the best the world has known, used to find atolls by searching the sky for green-tinted clouds. At sea they also studied the flight of birds heading from their fishing grounds to their colonies to feed their young, and the men turned the prows of their seagoing canoes to follow. Now the birds were beginning to straggle back to Pearl and Hermes, carrying in their gullets and stomachs small fish and squid that they would regurgitate for their chicks.

Albatrosses feed largely on squid, and their digestive systems contain reservoirs of oily squid chowder. When a chick inserts its beak crosswise into its parent's beak the adult expels a jet of liquid that the chick catches so deftly that not a drop is spilled. Albatrosses continue to feed their young until they are five to six months old and almost ready to fly, and then abandon them. Thereafter the chicks, which drink salt water, may go without food for as long as two or three weeks, living on their body reserves. If they have not learned to fly and fend for themselves by then, they die. Many of those on Pearl and Hermes had already been abandoned and a man could tell almost at a glance which of them were going to live, and which not. The weaker birds would stand in one place day after day, scarcely moving, while the stronger would continue to exercise their wings preparing for their long flight out to sea.

Some of their short practice flights, however, ended in quick death. The chicks would land 20 or 30 yards offshore and while they drifted with outstretched wings sharks would drag them under. The annual feast of albatrosses had attracted to the island a large number of sharks,

Member of a species once found only on Laysan Island, a Laysan finch, shown nibbling seeds of setaria grass, is one of a growing colony introduced to Southeast Island on Pearl and Hermes Reef in 1967. The bird's right leg has been banded for identification. The island's only land birds, Laysan finches feed on insects and grass seeds. In choosing nesting grounds, they favour the dense matting of eragrostis grass on the island's sheltered side.

among them reef whitetips and tigers, which sometimes swam so close to the beach that their bellies appeared to rub the sand. A few years ago on Midway, sailors from the naval station caught a 16-foot tiger shark and strung it up on a pole to take its picture. After a couple of bushels of wet feathers had oozed out of the shark's mouth the sailors cut it open and found 13 young albatrosses inside.

Among the birds coming home to feed their young there were a number of boobies, so called because of their apparent stupidity, although that may not be quite the word to apply to them. The three species on Pearl and Hermes have a persecuted, frantic look that fits well with their names—the blue-faced booby and the red-footed booby, which are white, and the brown booby. The adults are about 18 inches tall and appear to be hard-working conscientious birds. By day they toil in their watery vineyard, dipping into it for squid and skimming over it to catch flying fish, and when they have a full basket for their chicks they try to get it home without being hijacked. They fly low, as though trying to escape the notice of the piratical frigate birds, but this is not much use. The frigates plunder them anyway.

Frigate birds, also called man-o'-war birds, are nearly as large as albatrosses although lighter, blackish in colour and with wingspreads that approach seven feet. They have long, deeply forked tails, which in flight they open and close like shears. They are absolute masters of the air, remaining aloft indefinitely by riding currents, although they can also perform acrobatics and can put on a handsome turn of speed. When the boobies and tropic birds come home loaded late in the day, the frigate birds dive down on them and sometimes even grab them, forcing them to cough up their catch. Before the falling fish or squid can hit the water the frigates swoop down and gobble it up. Luckily most boobies carry more than one fish. In *Birds of Hawaii* ornithologist George C. Munro quotes an observer who is "positive that [the booby] always gives up a flying fish to the frigate, retains a squid for its young and a flying fish for itself". Whatever the case, the look of the boobies is not so much one of stupidity as of extreme exasperation verging on lunacy.

Frigate birds have their own problems. I watched one commit a mid-air robbery and take the fish home to its own chick. The frigate glided in, braked, hovered over the nest and then collapsed on it like a broken umbrella. After countless generations of airborne existence the legs and feet of frigate birds are atrophied, weak and useless except for perching. The birds cannot walk. When they land they must come down on a spot with some elevation, however slight, so that they can take off again without the aid of an upwards push with their legs. Their great wings can make the most of the smallest updraught, but if they chance to land on a flat place on a calm day they must do a great deal of flapping and floundering before they can become airborne once more.

After dinner Marvin Cunningham, the Navy hospitalman, said that he had found a dead seal, and we walked over to have a look at it. The animal had been dead for a couple of months and there was no longer much odour. It was on the coral-reef side of the island, lying in a few inches of water in a tiny protected cove. Small waves, only a few inches high, had been lapping at the carcass and had neatly separated most of what remained of the flesh from the bones, so that Cunningham's task was mainly to gather them up and put them in a huge plastic bag. The action of the waves had detached some of the smaller bones and teeth from the skeleton. Cunningham searched carefully for them in the water, meanwhile talking about the unusual characteristics of seals.

Seals can dive to remarkable depths—a few have been caught by accident on fishhooks as far as 500 feet or more under water. One reason for their remarkable swimming ability is that most seals are so streamlined; they have no protuberances anywhere. The sex organ of the male is recessed and can be thrust out through a slit in the body when needed. To assist in this the seal has a baculum, or penis bone, that is also found in some other mammals, although not in the primates. It is not firmly attached by ligaments to other bones and thus it can readily become separated from the rest of the skeleton. In the case of Cunningham's seal this had already happened and he looked right and left for the bone in the shallows. "We can't send an incomplete skeleton to a museum," he said.

"God forbid," said a co-worker, joining in the search.

At length Cunningham found the bone, which resembled a small ivory pencil, and put it in the plastic bag with the others. When he got the skeleton back to Midway Island he would put fresh water and detergent in the bag, and after some soaking, scrubbing and drying it would be ready to pack and ship.

Night, in contrast to the shattering dawn, seems to fall slowly in the mid-Pacific. It takes the stars a long time to drill holes in the sky. When it was dark Kridler made another patrol of the island. On the beach, barely visible against the sand, hundreds of little nocturnal ghost crabs glided back and forth. The flimsy tower with its guano-covered jerry can loomed like a scaffold. The sooty terns, which fly all night calling out their other name, "wideawake, wideawake, wideawake," swooped low overhead. As we approached the grassy centre of the island Kridler stopped, listening. At first I could hear only the noise of the terns but then beneath it emerged a hair-raising sound, exactly like the sound of men and women, barely conscious, in agony. There were long-drawn-out feminine moans answered by masculine groans; wordless noises of heartbreak and grief; mournings, wailings and low lamentations. Certainly no other birds, and probably no other living creatures except humans, make such sounds. It was a colony of tunnel-digging shearwaters. They were singing.

In the morning Kridler and Cunningham set out to tag some seal pups. Hawaiian monk seals come ashore on Pearl and Hermes and other refuge islands throughout the year. Like humans, they are fond of wriggling on the sand until they have made a comfortable pillow and bed, where they doze in the warm sun. They are trusting creatures who have no enemies but man on land, and in the sea only the shark. A man can approach within four or five feet of them before they show any alarm, and even then they merely grumble about being disturbed and do not become belligerent. Females with pups will roar and try to bite anyone who threatens their pups, but this is not very surprising. The faces of the seals seem wise and pensive, with drooping whiskers and sad eyes. They appear to be weeping, and in fact they are. Unlike most mammals, seals have no tear ducts to drain off internally the fluid that lubricates their eyes. Instead, the fluid overflows externally, rolling down their cheeks in streams of seeming sorrow.

When seal pups are born they weigh about 35 pounds and are covered with beautiful glossy black fur, for which they would be clubbed to death if hunters could get at them. They grow at an incredible rate, drinking huge quantities of milk, and may reach weights of 200 pounds within six to seven weeks, after which they are weaned. Once on their own, they shrink to perhaps 100 pounds and begin an orderly growth until they become eight feet long and weigh 650 to 700 pounds. They moult their black baby fur six to seven weeks after birth, eventually becoming soft greyish brown above and light grey on their stomachs.

Kridler and his co-workers have been tagging seal pups since 1966 and have become very adept at it. There were a half-dozen pups on the beach with their mothers and he tagged each one in a matter of three or four minutes. Cunningham would distract the mother, waving his arms, jumping and shouting, while Kridler slipped in behind and quickly fastened a tag in the webbing of the pup's hind flipper. During this operation one of the pups became so far separated from its angry parent that it seemed safe enough to pick it up. I held the pup in my arms for a few moments, looking at its friendly unsuspicious face, and put it down when a big tear welled out of the corner of its eye. The pup hurried off to join its mother and the two immediately touched noses, which is apparently the seals' way of reassuring each other.

After the last of the pups had been tagged, we waited on the beach for the Navy helicopter from Midway to pick us up. An adult seal was swimming lazily about 50 feet offshore and Kridler was taking pictures of it. It was then that we saw the shark's fin cutting through the small waves, fast, in a straight line for the seal. Within seconds there was a thrashing in the shallow water where the two had met.

We wear, all of us, the old mammal school tie. Our blood is warm. We rarely think, until we see and become emotionally involved in a fight between a fellow mammal and a damned shark, just how strong our loyalty is. I glanced at Kridler, who was trying vainly to get pictures of the underwater struggle. He was yelling encouragement to the seal and so was I. We shouted until we were hoarse, both of us prejudiced, bloodthirsty mammalian chauvinists to the core.

What can a seal do against a shark? I had read that porpoises had been known to fight sharks. They form a ring around their enemy, and while a porpoise on one side of the ring makes a diversionary movement, another on the opposite side dashes in and rams the shark with the top of its head. In short order they batter the shark to death. But a lone seal? For an instant as I stared into the water I thought of *The Threepenny Opera* by that outstanding German mammal, Bertolt Brecht, and the translation, "When the shark bites with his teeth, dear/ Scarlet billows start to spread. . . ."

But there were no scarlet billows. God knows what the seal did to the shark, but after a few wild flurries the shark turned tail and swam off, beaten. The seal continued to laze along in the water, parallel with the beach, and then hauled itself ashore about 50 yards away. There was not a mark on her, or him. It is too much to think that the seal understood our cheering, any more than it understood the gigantic bird that soon came rattling down, swallowed us, and flew away.

A Teeming Speck in the Ocean

PHOTOGRAPHS BY DAVID CAVAGNARO

Far off the course of the ships that ply the Pacific, a mere speck in the ocean when seen from a passing jet, Pearl and Hermes Reef ranks high on any list of the world's most isolated places. Since 1822, when the wreck of the whalers *Pearl* and *Hermes* gave it its name and put it on the map, relatively few people have set foot there. The nearest landfall is Midway, 100 miles to the northwest. And although the reef is officially one of the Hawaiian Islands, Honolulu lies over 1,000 miles southeast.

But if human beings find Pearl and Hermes off the beaten path, other creatures do not. From the surrounding sea—itself incredibly rich in fish—seals and turtles lumber ashore; albatrosses, frigate birds and a dozen other winged species come wheeling in. All these visitors derive their sustenance from the ocean, but must touch down on dry land to fulfill critical parts of their life cycles. Pearl and Hermes Reef well serves their purpose, thanks to its very isolation and security—it has been part of the Hawaiian Islands National Wildlife Refuge since its creation in 1909.

Pearl and Hermes is not one reef but a series of them—a small atoll—forming a 15-mile-wide circle of coral around a lagoon whose waters fill the site of a sunken volcano. Most of the atoll lies below the surface of the sea; the notable exception is a kidney-shaped 31-acre tract of coral and sand known as Southeast Island, which stands only 12 feet above sea level at its highest point.

Southeast Island, where most of the photographs on the following pages were taken, is no paradise for the creatures that tenant it. The climate is mostly hot and dry; the island is steadily whipped by trade winds, tempered only occasionally by brief tropical showers. Salinity poses a constant threat of dehydration. The only plants that survive are grasses and vines that retain a large quantity of water in their leaves. Though scrawny, they provide a dense matting that helps to anchor the thin blanket of sand on the coral.

Each in its own way, the species that use the island as a base adapt to its living conditions. The birds, for example, have learned to tip their beaks up to catch a life-sustaining sip of rain; some use the plant matting as nesting places. Whatever their distinctive habits, seals, turtles and sea birds alike return periodically to the island to court, breed, nest, hatch, raise young—and thus perpetuate their kind.

A helicopter view of part of Pearl and Hermes Reef reveals its three distinct environments. In the foreground is the shallow lagoon, a lighter hue than the deep ocean (background). The third component, coral, appears in the form of a barrier reef, causing a white line of breakers, and as sand on Southeast Island, seen jutting into the lagoon.

A SCHOOL OF MANINI SWIMMING OVER PORITES CORAL

Life and Death
in the Lagoon

The lagoon of Pearl and Hermes Reef is less than 10 feet deep in places, yet its shoals harbour a huge and diverse population of butterfly fish, parrot fish, starfish, squid, sea urchins and the ever-present black-striped manini (*left*). About nine inches long when mature, the manini belongs to the surgeonfish family, so called for the scalpel-like spine they use as a weapon of defence. Like the manini, which feeds on algae, most of its neighbours are also grazers, sustained by the detritus that drifts down through the underwater coral reefs, which are built up of the skeletons of tiny creatures such as porites and pocillopora.

Off limits to fishing and to the oystering once pursued there, the lagoon shields its own against all but their natural foes. A swooping sea bird nabs a fish venturing near the surface; doom also lurks in the form of large fish—*ulua* and tiger sharks—that invade from the ocean via breaks in the barrier reef. The shark, omnivorous in its tastes, will make a pass at anything alive in the lagoon —seals and turtles in transit, an underwater photographer—but will settle for mouthfuls of the little lagoon dwellers.

In these harsh but necessary relationships between predator and prey, the waters of Pearl and Hermes Reef help preserve the delicate life-and-death balance ordained by nature, free of the upsets that human interference would bring.

MONK SEAL DEFENDING ITS PUP AT A VISITOR'S APPROACH

A Secluded Shore for a Seal Nursery

The Hawaiian monk seal, named for the cowl-like skin fold at the back of its neck, is only one of two species of seal that live permanently in tropical waters. (The other is the elephant seal.) The monk seal is faring particularly well at Pearl and Hermes Reef and all through the Hawaiian Islands National Wildlife Refuge —in conditions not shared by its kin elsewhere. In the Mediterranean declining numbers of the species have been driven back to a few small islands by man's encroachment, and in the Caribbean a lone pair of monk seals was last seen in 1949.

Even the Hawaiian seals were hunted to near-extinction by 19th Century sealers for their fur, meat and oil. By 1900 the monk-seal population in this area of the Pacific had dwindled to less than 100. When the Hawaiian wildlife refuge was established, they acquired a new lease on life, and now number about 1,500. Pearl and Hermes, with its smooth, sandy, isolated beaches, is one of their principal pupping grounds.

Monk seals mate once a year, but the cow bears young—a single pup —only every other year. This curious circumstance results from the fact that mating takes place soon after pupping time, but cows that have just given birth cannot conceive until the breeding season is past; since their pregnancy spans 11 months, they produce offspring in alternate years—a natural and automatic form of population control.

A SEAL PUP NURSING

A YOUNG ADULT RELAXING ON THE BEACH

The Behemoth of the Beach

On any given day the coral sand beach at Southeast Island may be host to half a dozen or so giant green turtles. Having fed at sea on algae and seaweed, they come ashore to sleep—sometimes for days.

The turtle population on the beach increases somewhat from May to July as females arrive to lay their eggs. While they nest only every third year they do so on a grand scale, each depositing 400 to 500 eggs in the process. After seven weeks of incubation in the gentle heat of the sand, hatchlings make an instinctive dash for the lagoon, running a gauntlet of predatory frigate birds. Once in the water, they are prey to sharks and *ulua*; only two per cent of them reach maturity.

Despite this low rate of survival, a turtle herd can maintain or even increase its numbers because those that do survive can live a century or more. Their longevity depends to a certain extent on their wanderlust, or lack of it. Green turtles have been known to roam the Pacific for distances of as much as 600 miles. The more they travel the more they are likely to end up as turtle meat, a gourmet delicacy. The state of Hawaii has no closed season on turtle hunting, and no restrictions on the number or size that may be captured. But the secluded waters of the wildlife refuge provide the turtles with reasonable security against poaching, and currently about 1,000 of them enjoy its protection.

ABOUT 300 POUNDS OF GREEN SEA TURTLE, HEAD ON

A SPHINX MOTH REPOSING ON SETARIA GRASS

A Precarious Foothold for Plants and Insects

The fact that there are plants and insects at all at Pearl and Hermes is a miracle of nature. Vegetation is vital to the islands of the atoll because it anchors the sand and provides nesting shelter for many sea birds. Yet prevailing conditions conspire to thwart the growth of all but the hardiest plants. Fresh water is available only from occasional tropical showers. Average tides rise two feet, washing over the mostly flat ground and dappling it with salt.

Seeds borne by the trade winds and the birds take hold only if they are of plant species that are endowed with fleshy leaves to store water and hairy surfaces to retard evaporation. Setaria grass is one of the handful of plants that have managed to establish themselves and another, perhaps the most successful, is the puncture vine. In 1931 only one of its seedlings was reported on Southeast Island; today it is a mainstay of higher ground there, which it covers with a dense matting.

Among the few insects that have triumphed over the vicissitudes of life on the atoll are the miller moth and the sphinx moth. A particularly remarkable adaptation was made by the sphinx moth. It is equipped with a long tongue to collect the nectar deep inside trumpet-shaped flowers —none of which grow on Southeast Island. As a result, it has learned to feed on the puncture vine's unfurled buds, which resemble the sphinx moth's favoured trumpet blooms.

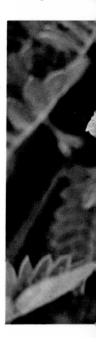

A SPHINX-MOTH CATERPILLAR

PUNCTURE VINE IN FULL BLOOM

A MILLER MOTH ON A PUNCTURE VINE

FLEDGLING ALBATROSSES START LEARNING TO FLY

A Serene Haven for Sea Birds

Legions of sea birds (*left and overleaf*) have turned Pearl and Hermes into one gigantic rookery. By the tens of thousands, albatrosses, terns, boobies, tropic birds, shearwaters, noddies and other species claim just about every square inch of available nesting space. The shearwaters, in fact, raise their chicks in burrows underground, thus creating a double-decker kind of hatchery.

Because the adult birds feed themselves and their young on marine animals such as flying fish and squid, there is perpetual swarming overhead as they commute between water and nest. A human visitor can take few steps without the risk of being buzzed by an incoming tern, sinking knee-deep in a nesting burrow or crushing a newly laid egg. In fact, he can even reach up and pluck a bird right out of the air.

In all the apparent chaos there is, however, some order. Each species of bird stakes out a different area for its nesting ground. On Southeast Island, for example, black-footed albatrosses tend to hang around the beach; the Laysan albatrosses favour the grassy stretches farther inland. Sooty terns flock by the tidal basin; white fairy terns perch separately on craggy coral. Blue-faced, or masked, boobies prefer the bare coral beach; their red-footed cousins build their nests on higher ground amid the puncture vines. The shearwaters, in a sense, have the best of it: an underground kingdom all their own.

A NODDY TERN BROODING IN ERAGROSTIS GRASS

A WEDGE-TAILED SHEARWATER IN ITS BURROW

MASKED BOOBIES AND CHICK

A RED-TAILED TROPIC BIRD

A FAIRY TERN RESTING ON CORAL

A RED-FOOTED BOOBY WITH ITS FLUFFY YOUNG

Converging from every point on the horizon, sooty terns head back for Pearl and Hermes Reef at sunset after a long and vigorous day

of ocean fishing. Their stomachs are replete with squid and small fish, which they will regurgitate and feed to their waiting nestlings.

5/ The Swamp on the Mountain

Most beautiful, most blessed Kauai.
Serene she rests, rising from the sea
To lift the leaf-bud of her mountain Waialeale
To the sky— ANCIENT HAWAIIAN CHANT

The raindrop that struck John Sincock on the forehead came at him from a great distance, perhaps 2,000 miles or more horizontally across the north Pacific from the general direction of San Francisco. It did not start out in life as a raindrop, of course, but as an invisible waft of warm humidity like the breath of a girl whispering in a man's ear. However, by the time it reached John Sincock it had become liquid, was tearing along at perhaps 30 or 40 miles an hour and struck him smartly about an inch above his right eye.

The raindrop would never have hit him if it had not been for an array of coincidences. If John Sincock had not been a wildlife biologist; if he had not been searching for birds of ineffable rarity; if the trade winds had not been blowing briskly; if the topography of the island of Kauai had not been just what it is; if his work had not taken him to the top of Mount Waialeale; if. . . . But the drop *did* hit him, so it is less worthwhile to muse about what might have been than to consider how the drop flew with pinpoint accuracy all that distance and collided with his brow.

The trade winds blow from the general direction of North America out to the Hawaiian Islands and beyond them, mixing with other winds, to the Philippines and China. As they pass over the water the trades become laden with humidity. When the air becomes excessively damp it rains at random on the sea. The low islands of the Hawaiian chain, Midway for example, depend upon such scattered showers. The low islands cannot reach up and snag passing clouds; they must passively accept whatever rainfall they are lucky enough to get, which may be only 15 to 20 inches in a year. But the high Hawaiian islands have mountains on them, and therein lies the meteorological rub. The mountains grab the clouds, so to speak, and wring them out like sponges. The rainfall is unbelievable. John Sincock was standing on the rainiest place on earth.

The trade winds approach Hawaii from the north-northeast or northeast. When they strike a mountain they must rise to pass over it, and as they ascend into cooler air their moisture condenses into rain. Maximum rainfall occurs at an altitude somewhere between 4,000 and 7,000 feet; above that, the fall tapers off because the winds are less moist. The lower slopes of Mauna Loa on the island of Hawaii are very damp indeed, with patches of dripping fern jungle; but its 13,680-foot summit is a stone desert. And the rainfall occurs mostly on the windward side of a mountain; to leeward it is arid. However, these are only general principles to which there are always exceptions.

The shape of a mountain, the aspect it presents to the oncoming wind, also affects the amount of rainfall and where it comes down. There are places in Hawaii where the northeast trades are opposed at right angles by *pali*, or cliffs, running southeast. A perpendicular opposition of this sort is formed by the Koolau Mountains on the island of Oahu. The *pali* rise in places as much as 1,500 feet; when the wind encounters those cliffs head on it rushes upwards with terrific force. At one point often visited by tourists on the Pali Highway the updraught is so strong that the bus drivers jocularly advise their passengers not to try to commit suicide by jumping off the cliffs because their bodies would only be blown back up. That is not strictly true, but smaller objects such as coins do sometimes return in the upcurrent. Not far from the lookout point there is an upside-down waterfall: as the stream flows over the cliff the water often falls up instead of down. Raindrops too are blown upwards. Instead of landing on the windward side of the mountains most of them fall slightly to leeward of the summit ridge.

On the island of Kauai, Mount Waialeale places similar steep cliffs in the path of the trades, but the situation is compounded by a couple of factors. The summit of Waialeale is nearly a mile high (5,080 feet), reaching up into the middle of the cool zone where maximum rainfall occurs. It also happens that some long valleys, coming in from the side and narrowing upwards, accelerate and funnel the wind towards the top of Waialeale. As a result, tons and tons of water fall there all the time.

On the beaten-down, bastinadoed summit region no vegetation can grow much more than a foot high. In many places there is only bare, sticky grey clay from which the water runs off as fast as it falls, giving rise to a dozen streams that radiate downwards to make Kauai what it is called: the Garden Island. Just to the northwest, leeward of the summit, there begins an irregularly shaped, wooded plateau, about nine miles by two or three, known as the Alakai Swamp. It is in the Alakai that the rare birds live, and it is there that John Sincock was walking when he was hit by the raindrop that had his number on it.

It has long been known that it is very wet on Waialeale; the top of the mountain is almost always covered by a boiling mass of rain clouds like the head of an old politician slumbering under towels in a barbershop. At infrequent intervals, usually in the early morning, the clouds part long enough for a helicopter to nip up to the summit carrying Sincock and a companion or two, perhaps a few interested visitors or a team of men from the U.S. Geological Survey who go there to read the rain gauges.

Although men have been keeping track of rainfall elsewhere in the world for centuries it was only in 1910 that the U.S.G.S. began its efforts to find out what it amounts to on Waialeale. In that year an engineer and some helpers managed to place a 50-gallon galvanized can near the summit after carrying and rolling it up through the Alakai Swamp. The Hawaiian rain gods smiled and spat in the can. It overflowed. Next year a gauge that would measure nearly 12 feet of rainfall was installed, and the gods chuckled and filled it up. In 1915 another gauge, a whopper capable of recording 25 feet, was somehow hauled up to the summit; the gods laughed aloud and slapped their thighs and the gauge overflowed. By this time the engineers were beginning to glimpse the size of the problem, and in 1920 they installed the mother of all gauges. Essentially it too was only a metal can but it was as big around as a windmill tank. It had a small opening at the top and it could record 990 inches—more than 82 feet—of rainfall. The gods stopped laughing and settled down to do a little serious raining but, perhaps because they were getting old or overconfident, they were unable to fill the tank in one year. The engineers rejoiced and at last began to collect some accurate figures. However, they had overlooked a detail, as engineers sometimes do. They had forgotten to install a spigot at the bottom of the tank so that it could be easily drained. In order to empty the tank it was necessary to tip it over; the tank soon buckled, began to leak and became useless.

In 1928 a reinforced, bottom-draining 900-inch gauge was lugged up the mountain and installed, and the struggle was over. The gauge served until 1949 when, in the first use of helicopters for that purpose, a new-fangled instrument was flown to the summit. Today an occasional hardy hunter of pigs or goats still fights his way to the mountaintop on foot, but most men who have any business up there go by aircraft. The era of manhandling gauges through the swamp is gone, and small loss. The task was almost unbelievably brutal. Indeed, even the task of carrying a heavy weight *down* from Waialeale was difficult in the extreme. In 1948 a U.S.G.S. engineer died of a heart attack about 300 yards from the summit; although he had six companions they could not muster the strength to drag his body any distance. So they tied it up in a tree to protect it from pigs, which would have eaten it, and went to seek help. It took a party of 16 men three days to carry the body down.

What *is* the rainfall on Waialeale? The National Weather Service in Honolulu computes the average at 486 inches, well over 40 feet, per year. In the record year of 1948 there were 624.1 inches, a foot of rain every week. (New York City averages 44 inches a year; San Francisco, 20 inches; Phoenix, 8 inches.) Partisans of various localities, notably those of a place called Cherrapunji in the hills of Assam in India, dispute the idea that Waialeale is the rainiest spot on earth. However, their arguments do not hold water. It does rain in Cherrapunji—900 inches were once recorded there in a year, and 150 inches in five days. But the big rains of Cherrapunji occur during the monsoon season; at other times it is relatively dry, so that the yearly average is only 450 inches. That is 36 inches less than the yearly average on Waialeale, where it rains heavily in all seasons. Actually, in measuring such prodigious downpourings it is not possible to be more than approximately correct. The wind on Waialeale often blows the rain horizontally across the summit, affecting the amount caught in the gauge. If the gauge were moved or perhaps screened, the catch would be greater or less. The situation is the same in Cherrapunji, Luzon, Nigeria, Tahiti and indeed in another of the Hawaiian Islands, Maui, where as many as 578 inches of rain have been recorded in a year on the summit of 5,788-foot Puu Kukui. In any case let us agree that Waialeale is as wet as any place on the planet and let it go at that.

It must be admitted that the raindrop that struck John Sincock on Waialeale, even though it had his number on it, was not a very special raindrop. Sincock had been hit by 247,047,276 other drops, more or

less, all addressed to him c/o General Delivery, Alakai Swamp, where he spends a lot of time. He is a government man employed in the Endangered Species Program, Bureau of Sport Fisheries and Wildlife, U.S. Department of the Interior. Before taking a look at the swamp through Sincock's eyes it is worth taking a quick look at Sincock himself. Like other government employees encountered in this book—Eugene Kridler refusing to cheat on the number of transects he walked on Pearl and Hermes Reef, or Donald Peterson looking down the throat of a volcano —Sincock is a good man. In the army he would be walking the point, the one who leads a squad on patrol and gets shot at first. Behind him there would be a constantly widening train of fat PX clerks and golf-playing generals, but Sincock would be out on the point or, in this case, thrashing through the swamp.

Sincock's work, which is to him a great if often hazardous pleasure, is to search for rare birds and find out all he can about their lives and habits. In this pursuit he has passed five years on Kauai and has made scores of expeditions, almost always alone, into the Alakai Swamp. He knows the place as well as any living man and has even become grudgingly fond of it, his old adversary. A few years ago on the occasion of his second marriage he flew to the wild wet summit with his fiancée and a minister and the ceremony was performed up there. In appearance Sincock is remote from the cartoonist's impression of the vaguely effeminate bird watcher. He is a strong, uncommonly handsome dark-haired man in his early forties; in the old days in Hollywood central casting might have typed him as a white hunter.

Sincock does not spend much time on the rain-battered summit of Waialeale because that is not where the birds are, although he often pauses to look at the ruined stone foundation of a small temple built there long ago by the Hawaiians. The rain gods and a good many others—one ancient chant refers to "the four hundred thousand elves, the countless host of sprites, rank upon rank of woodland gods"—once inhabited or visited the top of the mountain. Today there are some Hawaiians who believe the gods are still there, perhaps in greater number than before. Like the native birds, the gods have sought refuge from civilization by fleeing to higher and lonelier places. When Sincock passes the temple he invariably sees offerings of coins placed on the stones or tucked in chinks, many of them put there by true believers. He would not dream of pocketing the money but recently he picked up a coin to see how old it was. The date on it was 1971.

Ohia trees weave a tangle in Alakai Swamp, 4,000 feet up in the centre of Kauai; they are soaked by more than 400 inches of rain a year.

The windswept, treeless area of tussocks, dwarfed plants and grey clay, an open bog or mountain barren, extends for about a quarter of a mile downhill from the summit. Descending, Sincock enters the Alakai Swamp, which stretches off to the northwest. There the rainfall tapers gradually to amounts the mind finds easier to accept, perhaps 20 feet a year on the average, although Sincock once survived a day in the swamp when one of the rain gauges (several are in place now) recorded some 40 inches in 24 hours. "Swamp" is the term universally applied to the place but that is more a matter of convenience than of fact. The Alakai is a high plateau, bounded on three sides by cliffs, with an altitude of about 4,200 feet—well above the range of the fearsome *Culex* mosquito. There are a few flat areas in it and even some little pools, but generally the terrain is sloping. In several places it has been deeply gashed by the streams which have their origin near by, with the result that there are dizzying ravines and knife-edged ridges. "There are places," Sincock says, "where I can walk along a ridge top that is only a few feet wide with a drop-off of 500 feet on both sides." The ravines carry off the rainfall rapidly, draining the swamp much faster than one might expect. A layer of peaty muck covers much of it to a depth of perhaps a foot, and here and there a man can sink to his waist in it, but the Alakai is nothing like the Okefenokee.

It is very easy to get lost in the Alakai. When it is not actually raining the air is full of thick white mist. The sky is toadbelly grey, the colour of a January afternoon, rarely offering a glimpse of the sun or stars. The mainlander's idea that moss grows thickest on the shady (north) side of trees will be of no help in orienting him here. Light green moss grows luxuriantly on all sides and branches of the trees, coating and upholstering them to incredible thickness. A man may grasp what appears to be a sturdy moss-covered branch as big around as his forearm, squeeze it, and see water spurt in all directions while a cold stream pours down inside his sleeve. The branch beneath the moss may be no thicker than the wire in a coat hanger.

With plastic tape Sincock has marked a couple of tracks or trails for his own use, and there are a few well-nigh invisible paths known only to Hawaiians and perhaps to the gods of white mist gliding through the white fog, but an alien in the Alakai would not last long. There are tales of men who ought to have known better, hunters who have vanished leaving no trace except rifles that turned to thin streaks of rust on the peat. "On the mainland," Sincock says, "the general rule when you are lost is to follow a stream until it gets you out somewhere. But here if you follow a stream it will only lead you to a high waterfall pouring over a precipice. You have to follow the ridges, not the streams." It is useless to follow tracks used by animals; often worse than useless. "Once when I had been in the swamp for about a week I was down on my stomach in the muck, crawling under a fallen tree, when I came face to face with a pig. He was so close I could smell his breath. Meanest goddam pig I ever saw, about 300 pounds, with big yellow tusks. One of us had to get out of the way, so I started to back up to oblige him. But do you know, I looked worse and smelled worse than the pig did, so *he* backed up to get out of my way." Sometimes Sincock encounters goats in the Alakai, huge (for Hawaii), ugly creatures that weigh as much as a grown man. Because they spend all their lives walking on mud and peat, with no hard surfaces to keep their hooves in trim, their feet are splayed almost to the size of saucers.

The swamp is covered by a mixed forest dominated by red-flowered *ohia*. In their extremely adaptive fashion they are able to grow to maturity, 11 or 12 inches tall, in the summit barren. Farther down among the ridges and ravines they may reach 30 to 40 feet although the average is less, well below the heights of 100 or more they attain in favourable locations. The knee-high forms are called *ohia makenoe*, little *ohia* of the mist. Second among the trees is an endemic species called *lapalapa*, which is found only in the high, wet ground of the Alakai and the rainy heights of the Koolau range on Oahu. The *lapalapa* has several curious characteristics. When any part of the tree is bruised it emits a strong odour of carrots; its wood will burn when green, a providential circumstance that may have saved a few lost souls in the near-freezing temperatures of the swamp; and *lapalapa* leaves, somewhat like those of the quaking aspen of the mainland, are constantly in motion even in breezes so slight as to be imperceptible to men. The tree's name is related to the Hawaiian *hula*, whose performers were divided into two groups—the *olapa* (agile ones) and the *ho'opaa* (steadfast ones). The *olapa* were young men and women who could best illustrate the grace and beauty of the human form by dancing, while the *ho'opaa* were older people who handled the heavier musical instruments and played their parts while kneeling or sitting. "The *hula* you are likely to watch in night clubs or on hotel terraces," Sincock says, "are pretty sad corruptions of what was once an important art form. To the Hawaiians it combined poetry, religion, drama and dance, opera and literature. It had practically no relation to the sexy hip-shaking you see today." Whatever the case, the *olapa* dancers and the moving tree can claim some kinship.

Sincock encounters all manner of improbable plants in the swamp, but as an ornithologist, not a botanist, he studies them mainly as they relate to birds. Thus when he passes an *ape ape* (pronounced *ah-pay ah-pay*) he merely blinks in astonishment and moves on. The plant is slightly shorter than a man, with huge kidney-shaped leaves as much as three feet or more in diameter. They serve admirably as umbrellas. The plant's rhubarb-like stalk, perhaps six inches thick, can be cut with one swipe of a machete.

When he first began to search for rare birds in the swamp, Sincock tried to catch them in Japanese mist nets for the purpose of banding them and checking them for diseases. These nets are woven of extremely fine nylon threads, almost invisible at close range, and measure about 40 by 10 feet. They are stretched between trees in areas where birds, funnelled there by the surrounding terrain, are likely to fly. Striking the nets, the birds drop into longitudinal pouches from which they cannot easily escape. "Mist nets may be excellent in dry country," Sincock says, "but in the Alakai they quickly become covered with dew, like huge spiderwebs, and the birds can see them. I *have* caught a lot of birds in the nets, but seldom a really rare one, and I don't use them much any more."

Although he does not employ the bird-catching method used by the old Hawaiians and other woodland people elsewhere, Sincock has a grudging admiration for its practicality. The Hawaiians merely smeared twigs or scaffold-like artificial perches with sticky substances made of viscous tree sap, gum, pitch or whatever was available, and when the birds alighted they were caught. The Hawaiians often ate songbirds, perhaps as many as four-and-twenty at one sitting in the manner of English royalty, but their most interesting use of small birds was to pluck their feathers to make brilliantly coloured capes, full-length cloaks and ornamental helmets (*right*). These beautiful objects rivalled, perhaps even surpassed the cloaks of ermine and sable, velvet and cloth of gold once made for European and Russian monarchs. Captain Cook, who was given some cloaks and helmets on his first visit to the islands, considered them very elegant and remarked that "the surface might be compared to the thickest and richest velvet, which they resemble, both as to the feel, and the glossy appearance".

The predominant colours of Hawaiian cloaks were red, from the *iiwi* and *apapane* birds; yellow, from the *o-o* and *mamo*; black, from var-

The royal emblems of an 18th Century Hawaiian chief included this handsome helmet and cape covered with the feathers of birds of the Alakai Swamp —the apapane, o-o and iiwi. The feathers—bright reds and yellows —were tied to mesh underlinings that were finely woven from vine roots.

ious birds, and more rarely, green, from the *ou*. The feathers were tied in tiny bunches and applied in overlapping rows, somewhat like roofing shingles, to a base of fine netting. The cloaks were worn only by chiefs and kings on ceremonial occasions and during battles—a few successful warriors thus accumulated several cloaks from their fallen enemies. The making of a large cloak required many years and an enormous number of feathers, which were supplied by the common people as part of their taxes. A cloak that belonged to King Kamehameha I, now in the Bishop Museum in Honolulu, contains some 500,000 golden feathers taken from at least 80,000 birds. In this case the birds were now-extinct *mamo*, a species endemic to the island of Hawaii, which were dark blue-black with a few yellow feathers on their thighs and above and below their tails. The birds were captured at the beginning of their moulting season, when perhaps a dozen of the most desirable feathers were plucked out and the *mamo* were released to grow new ones. The *iiwi* and *apapane* were a good deal less fortunate. They had so many red feathers that they could not have survived plucking, so they were first killed, then plucked and eaten.

The destruction of birds to make featherwork had little relation to their extinction or dwindling in number. Today both the *iiwi* and the *apapane* are fairly common in John Sincock's territory and he has no great concern with them beyond the pleasure he derives merely from their presence in the wild. The birds of particular importance to him are so rare that some of them have been seen only three or four times in this century. Most of them are *Drepanididae*—honeycreepers (*page 87*)—in the Alakai Swamp but there are several others elsewhere in Kauai that Sincock worries about. One of them is the *koloa*, a mallard-like duck once common on most of the Hawaiian islands. Today he encounters a few of them scattered along high mountain streams and occasionally spots one in an irrigation ditch or reservoir. He thinks about 2,500 of them are still alive on Kauai, and that this population is barely holding its own. There are also about 1,500 Hawaiian stilts, handsome black-and-white birds about 18 inches tall with long, pink reedlike legs. They live in coastal sloughs and lagoons that are constantly being eyed as landfill projects and thus, because the value of Hawaiian waterfront property is on a trajectory similar to that of Apollo 17, their survival is not necessarily assured.

In its habits the most unusual bird in Sincock's region, and no doubt among the most unusual in the world, is the *ao*, a sea bird known in Eng-

Cladonia skottsbergia, a delicate lichen, grows in the Alakai Swamp amid glossy-leaved Broussaisia arguta, a ground cover.

lish as Newell's Manx Shearwater and in Latin as *Puffinus puffinus new-elli*. It is pigeon-sized, glossy black above and pure white underneath. At one time it was fairly abundant in the major islands but by about 50 years ago it had become very rare. Like other shearwaters it nests in burrows, and it is thought that on Hawaii, Maui and Molokai it had been wiped out by mongooses, which could get at it in its nest. On Kauai, however, small numbers of *ao* continued to be seen, particularly on autumn nights when they crash-landed on illuminated highways, buildings and football fields. After landing they seemed unable, even though uninjured, to take off again.

It did not seem unusual to Sincock that the *ao* might be dazzled by light or that, like other sea birds downed on land, they should have difficulty in regaining flight; what excited him was the idea that somewhere on Kauai they might have a nesting site. No one had seen an *ao*'s burrow, egg or chick in many years, and if there was indeed a nesting colony it was doubtless in a place so wild that no naturalist had ever been there. It was possible, Sincock thought, that the birds could still breed in some remote area because Kauai, alone among the major islands, has no mongooses. One widely accepted explanation of this is that a shipment of the creatures, destined for rat-catching service in Kauai's cane fields, actually reached the island some 70 years ago but was kicked overboard by an angry man whose finger had been badly bitten when he stuck it into the crate. Another version of this story is that a few citizens of Kauai, fearful of the harm mongooses might do, organized a Mongoose Party along the lines of the Boston Tea Party. In any case, there are no mongooses on the island to devour the eggs and young of ground-nesting birds.

Sincock found an *ao* nesting site by following an odd scrap of information offered by a local pig hunter. While searching for his dogs after a hunt in a state forest reserve the man had found them coming down from the top of a 1,400-foot ridge east of the Alakai Swamp, and had been surprised to see that the dogs had black and white feathers in their mouths. Hmm, thought Sincock, imagining what might be up there. He soon arranged for a helicopter to drop him on top of the ridge, accompanied by naturalist Gerald Swedberg from the Hawaiian State Division of Fish and Game. "There was a pretty thick canopy of *ohia* trees on parts of the ridge," Sincock says, "and everywhere there was an impenetrable stand of *uluhe* fern about nine feet deep. The helicopter couldn't land, so we jumped. We hacked a trail along the top for about a quarter of a mile and then we began to hear *ao* calling from their burrows, dozens of them."

There were eggs, nestlings and adult birds in the colony, but Sincock and Swedberg could make no accurate count of them. "The ridge sloped off at about sixty-five degrees and it was very wet and slippery. Not a good place for climbing." After nightfall the adults in the burrows were joined by their mates, which had been fishing far out at sea and were returning with stomachs full of squid. "Some of the homecoming birds came down in the damnedest way," Sincock says. "They would circle overhead in the dark, making a loud, nasal sound that combined jack-ass braying and crow calling, and then—I assume deliberately—they would crash into the tops of the *ohia* trees and tumble down through the branches onto the jungle of ferns. After that they would claw their way down to the ground and start hunting for their burrows. Sometimes it would take a bird half an hour to find its nest."

Sincock and Swedberg watched the *ao* for several days and nights, concluding that there were perhaps 500 of them in the colony. Early one morning in the first light of dawn Sincock saw the silhouette of an *ao* against the sky and found the answer to a question that had been puzzling him. "How do the birds get back up into the air? Well, the wind really comes whistling up the face of that ridge before sunrise, and all the birds have to do is climb up through the ferns, flap their wings once or twice, and they're flying."

The rediscovery of the nesting grounds of Newell's Manx Shearwater was worth an article in *The Condor*, one of the foremost ornithological journals in the United States. Eventually Sincock will have another article, or perhaps several, on what he has been doing up in the Alakai Swamp for five years. In its learned, scientific way *The Condor* will not be interested in his personal hardships. Once, while intently following the call of a bird, he fell 30 feet into a ravine and smashed a leg so badly that the thought of gangrene and death flickered through his mind. He bound the leg with the plastic tape he uses to mark his trails, dragged himself out into an open place and lay down in the rain, hoping that sometime the sky would clear and a helicopter might come looking for him. By great good luck he was rescued after only two days, and after a couple of months he was able to walk without crutches. Today he carries flares and smoke bombs in the swamp but their value is perhaps more psychological than real. Sometimes the clouds press down on the ground for weeks at a time.

In winter it is bitterly cold in the Alakai. "I've been told that it snows up there," Sincock says, "although I've never seen it myself. The temperature drops into the low forties or high thirties, and in the rain and mist you can convince yourself that maybe you're going to freeze. Once I got so cold that I crawled into my little one-man tent and lit six candles I had with me. I was lying on my back like a corpse at a wake and I must have passed out for a little while. When I woke up it was raining like hell outside but, if you can believe it, the canvas floor of the tent was on fire from the candles." He doused the flames with rainwater and went back to sleep.

Sincock has verified, by personal observation, the existence of four exceedingly rare bird species in the Alakai—the *puaiohi* (small Kauai thrush), the Kauai *nukupuu*, the *ou* and the *o-o*. (Perhaps it is worth mentioning again that Hawaiian names did not sound laughable to the Hawaiians who invented them. The Hawaiians would have been convulsed, however, by such terms as robin or sparrow.) The most significant of Sincock's observations concerns the *o-o*, pronounced *oh-oh*, which he first saw on May 26, 1971. The bird, *Moho braccatus*, is small and generally dark in colour, slaty brown and black, with one striking feature—its thighs are rich golden yellow. It had last been sighted in 1963, and before that only a couple of times since 1900. After he had located the home territory of the *o-o* Sincock was able to observe the bird on several occasions, and soon found that there were three pairs of them in the vicinity. Two pairs were nesting in cavities in *ohia* trees, a discovery that seemed of importance to him. There were few such cavities available, as far as he could see, and he began to wonder what might happen if there were more. Accordingly he made 30 nesting boxes and in May 1972, he nailed them up in trees in various parts of the swamp. He did not expect the birds to use them—if they were to use them at all—until the boxes had become suitably weathered and natural in appearance. Perhaps, he thought, in about a year. . . .

Sincock keeps returning to the Alakai, watching and waiting, making notes, pursuing bird-calls up and down ridges and through dripping entanglements of ferns. He often slips and falls, gets lost in the mist and finds himself on the brink of cliffs. He walks with a barely noticeable limp and says that his leg is well healed and hurts only when it rains.

6/ The Enigma of a Tree

On this thoroughly explored planet almost all the larger species, from whales to watermelons, have been discovered by now. Scientists do find new creatures and plants every year but as a rule the discoveries are small, caught in the fine mesh of entomologists' or marine biologists' nets or observed growing in the shade of a pebble. In Hawaii the chances of encountering large new species are better than in Cincinnati, but few people expect to find anything as big as a tree. It is not likely that a plant of that size can have escaped all the professional botanists and informed laymen who have combed the islands.

Thus it was more than a little surprising to hear what the botanist, a man named Derral Herbst, was saying. Herbst, like my friend John Sincock the biologist, lives and works on the island of Kauai. We had fallen into a conversation about Hawaiian species, and in an unassuming way Herbst said that he and a fellow botanist, L. Earl Bishop, of the Honolulu Botanic Gardens, had recently discovered a new one.

Of what sort?

Herbst said that it was a tree.

A tree. I was sure I had heard him correctly and was so startled that the only reply I could make was that I hadn't heard people talking about it or seen any discussion of the discovery in the papers. It seemed, at least to me, that it was a fascinating piece of news. He shrugged. No reporters had come to inquire about it, and he is not the sort of man who would call them up and tell them. There is nothing unduly sus-picious or secretive about him; he merely sees no reason to answer questions no one has put to him. Ultimately the news would find its way into a proper botanical publication, where it might be spotted and possibly direct attention to him. But that would be a long time in the fu-ture. In order for a new plant species to be accepted by scientists a de-scription of it must be written in Latin and that, together with amplifications in a modern language, must be published in a botanical journal of impeccable standing. (The scientific tradition of writing in Latin today persists only in the field of botany. English is the universal language of the other sciences.) Such journals are glacial in their edi-torial movement. It sometimes requires months for a paper to get from one office to another across a six-foot hall. Herbst himself, when it comes to plant descriptions, is fairly glacial too.

"You have discovered a new tree and no one knows about it?"

"Well, of course, a few people. Other botanists."

I asked Herbst if he would be willing to show me the tree, and he said that he would indeed. "Earl Bishop and I discovered it only a few weeks ago, and I have seen it only once myself. It's down in the bottom of Waimea Canyon. We can easily walk there and back in two days." He had only two conditions: that I omit the Latin name that would be given to the tree, and that I avoid so detailed a description of its lo-cation that it might be found by a lunatic with an axe.

Derral Herbst, a South Dakotan in his mid-thirties who obtained his Ph.D. at the University of Hawaii, is the resident botanist at the Pacific Tropical Botanical Garden in Lawai, Kauai. The garden is being stocked with what seems likely to become the most comprehensive collection of tropical plants in the United States, to be used for research in con-servation, nutrition and medicine. Herbst spends part of his time in the garden and part of it searching for new plants in Hawaii and elsewhere in the Pacific. As we drove towards the canyon he told me something about his tree. He is a long way from the mid-continental prairie but still speaks with a quiet matter-of-factness that covers any excitement he may feel about the discovery. It is a flowering tree that belongs to the genus *Hibiscadelphus*, which is confined entirely to the Hawaiian Is-lands. The genus contains only a few species—Herbst's tree is the fifth —but it is a very interesting one that illustrates somewhat painfully how slender a hold on life many Hawaiian plants now have.

The word *Hibiscadelphus* was invented more than 60 years ago by the American naturalist Joseph Rock, a master of ornithology, botany and zoology who led expeditions into western China, Tibet and Cambodia on behalf of Harvard and the National Museum. In the early 1900s in Hawaii, Rock observed that there were three species of trees, two on the island of Hawaii and one on Maui, that at first glance appeared to be hibiscus but turned out to be quite different. Their flowers, instead of opening into the familiar broad, showy blooms of the hibiscus, were closed or furled even at maturity, curved tubes perhaps two inches long and half an inch in diameter. Because the trees were related to the hibiscus but distinct from it, Rock established them as a new genus called *Hibiscadelphus*, or brother of the hibiscus.

Rock saw his first species of *Hibiscadelphus* around 1910 while collecting botanical specimens with a friend, W. M. Giffard, and named it *Hibiscadelphus giffardianus*. Its flowers were deep magenta on the inside and greyish green outside. The tree itself was many-branched and low, perhaps 18 to 20 feet in height, with a trunk one foot in diameter. It was growing in the Kipuka Puaulu not far from Kilauea Volcano and was the last survivor of what may once have been a large number. "Unfortunately the tree", wrote Rock, "is the only one in existence. It is unique among all Hawaiian plants, and the author is sorry to relate that nothing has been done to protect it . . . it will succumb to the ravages of cattle, which inhabit a great many of our native forests."

The tree died in 1930 but shortly before its death some seeds were taken from it and planted on Giffard's estate several miles away. In 1936 the National Park Service reported that only two or three young trees were alive, "waging a losing fight against what is probably too damp a climate". Having come that close to extinction, the species was saved by transplanting and careful nursing and today a few score specimens exist in guarded cultivation. The second of the three species that Rock knew, *H. hualalaiensis*, was also found on the island of Hawaii on the slopes of another volcano, Hualalai. In 1912 he saw as many as a dozen individuals; a few still survive in the wild, protected from cattle by fences that may not last much longer. The tree has also been propagated, however, and exists in a few botanical gardens. The third of Rock's species, which he named *H. wilderianus* after another friend, Gerrit P. Wilder, once grew on the island of Maui. Here again Rock found only one tree, with young flowers that were yellow within and greenish yellow outside. Before it died Wilder himself collected seeds from the tree but succeeded in raising only one plant, which apparently perished before maturing. Since there is almost no chance that others have survived in the wild, the species is regarded as extinct.

Member of a rare Hawaiian genus of trees, a *Hibiscadelphus giffardianus* displays a fully mature bloom on a delicate branch. One of just five species belonging to the genus, *giffardianus* is nearly extinct, surviving only under closely protected cultivation. It is most obviously distinguished from its four *Hibiscadelphus* kin—named for the resemblance of their blooms to those of the hibiscus—by the shape, size and direction of its bracts, the leaflike structures at the base of the flower.

The fourth member of the remarkable genus was found—or rather, recognized—not in the wild but in the collection of dried plants in the herbarium of the Bernice P. Bishop Museum in Honolulu. It was placed in the collection in the 1860s, mistakenly classified as a hibiscus, but in 1920 a re-examination by the botanist Charles N. Forbes revealed it for what it was. Forbes named it *H. bombycinus*—the latter word means "silky" and probably refers to the fuzzy or hairy aspect of the tree. No specimen of *H. bombycinus* is known to survive; this species too is thought to have disappeared forever.

I asked Herbst if his discovery also consisted of a single tree. "No," he said. "There are six of them, growing fairly close together." For the past 10 minutes his car had been climbing steadily up the ridge road along the western rim of Waimea Canyon. At an altitude of about 3,000 feet he pulled the car off the road, locked it and we set out to walk down the Kukui Trail into the canyon. Although in places it is a trifle steep, as though it had been laid out by a shingler of Gothic roofs, the trail is an easy one and affords several magnificent views.

Waimea is often called the Grand Canyon of the Pacific, a remark that is not as pure chamber of commerce as it sounds. The two are somewhat alike in character, if not in size, and it is startling to come upon a gorge like Waimea on a small subtropical island. Although it is only 14½ miles long it is about 2,800 feet deep; its steep many-layered walls are beautifully coloured in the reds and ochres, blues and purples of the Grand Canyon itself; and here and there within it are erosion-carved shapes reminiscent of Arizona. However, Waimea receives more rainfall than the Grand Canyon and thus, except where its brightly painted slopes are too stony and steep to support it, contains much more vegetation. Waimea lies just to the west—and below—the high mountaintop swamp of the Alakai. Sparkling water pours down from the swamp into the canyon in thin never-ending streams with free falls of as much as 200 feet at a time.

We had descended only a short distance, following a path shaded by trees, when Herbst paused and pointed to a tangle of undergrowth. "Bush violet," he said, "*Viola tracheliifolia*." Pushing its way up out of the undergrowth, and partly supported by it, arose a woody stem, or trunk, about six feet high and at least an inch in diameter. Attached to it were shiny green leaves and pale bluish-white flowers readily recognizable as those of a violet. "It might be 10 or 12 feet tall if we straightened it out," he said. "It has to lean on other plants to stand up."

The violet was arborescent, or resembling a tree, as an adolescent resembles an adult. Arborescence occurs in several Hawaiian species, as it does among the plants of other oceanic islands such as the Galápagos, where sunflowers become trees 30 or 40 feet high. The ancestors of arborescent plants came of course from the mainlands, where their descendants still grow as relatively small, soft-stemmed herbs, while on islands many of the descendants have become tall and woody. There are assorted explanations for this startling behaviour, having to do with the sequence in which the plants arrived in Hawaii and exactly where they took hold. The forebears of the bush violet, for example, may have found a place available for them where there were no overshadowing forest trees or shrubs and may have taken advantage of the situation by gradually growing larger and larger. (With some conspicuous exceptions, the seeds of forest trees are generally heavier than those of violets, and perhaps for that reason take a longer time to travel.) It would have been a fairly normal evolutionary process, a fulfilling of the now-hackneyed old proposition that "if a niche opens up in nature, something will arise to fill it".

It is hard not to think of the blushing, six-foot violet of Hawaii in anthropomorphic terms. It is an ambitious plant. No doubt the ancestor of that violet opened its blue eyes and gazed with astonishment at the uninhabited landscape. "Hoo, boy!" it said. "Where are all those big, bullying trees?" Then it seized the main chance and began to grow as fast as it could. After 200,000 years it had become long and lank and could prop itself up on one elbow. After 500,000 it could get to its knees. After 700,000. . . . But suddenly the tall forest trees arrived, green trumpets blaring in the sky, and assumed their overshadowing place. The violet, which could almost but not quite stand up without help, leaned on a bush and murmured something that sounded like "Oh, shucks!" while a small blade of grass, which had timidly remained the same size during all those years, whispered, "Better luck next time".

We went deeper and deeper into the canyon and after a descent of nearly half a mile reached the river Waimea at the bottom. It is a small, slow river that can be crossed at many points by stepping and jumping along the smooth grey boulders in its bed. We followed the river for some distance, disturbing a black-crowned night heron that flew, perched and flew grudgingly ahead of us. Although there were recent footprints of men and horses in the sand, we saw no one. It was very quiet and the air was cool and still.

Mile-wide Waimea Canyon, called Hawaii's Grand Canyon, harbours a newly discovered species of Hibiscadelphus tree.

In midafternoon we came to a side canyon, the Koaie, that entered Waimea on the right. Herbst said the tree was up there. We entered the smaller canyon, pausing after a few minutes to drink from Koaie Stream. The water was tea coloured, rich with particles of vegetation washed down from the Alakai Swamp, and tasted clean and sweet. When we stood up after drinking and put on our packs again I looked at my watch: 3 o'clock. Unless something went wrong we would reach the tree in about an hour.

The side canyon was half a mile wide at its mouth but steadily narrowed as we went farther into it. The tall cliffs of reddish weathered lava on both sides were so nearly vertical that only a few small plants, dangling from cracks and crevices, clung to them. But down where we were walking, the trail ran along a talus of fallen rock covered with rich earth in which many trees were growing. There were *wiliwili*, which have claw-shaped flowers ranging in colour from pale red through orange and yellow to chartreuse. There were forest trees called *lama*, whose hard, reddish wood was used by the old Hawaiians in building *heiau*, or temples. Among them stood shiny-leaved coffee trees, long since escaped from cultivation, and big plants of sisal, also gone wild, with five-foot, 10-pound bayonet leaves and flower poles as much as 30 feet high. The predominant trees were *kukui*, the ground beneath them thickly covered with bony-shelled, greyish-black nuts about the size of walnuts. Another name for the *kukui* is candlenut; the oil-rich kernels were burned by the Hawaiians for illumination. A row of them would be strung on the stiff midrib of a coconut leaf to make a candle that was leaned against a stone. Each nut would burn for two or three minutes and then its neighbour would be ignited. In the evenings children were assigned to keep replacing the candles as long as light was wanted. Until recently there were still a few elderly Hawaiians who spoke of a light bulb as an electric *kukui*.

The path wandered up and down, sometimes rising far above the stream and sometimes dipping fairly close to it. The talus narrowed and widened. In places it had been terraced by the aboriginal Hawaiians to make platforms for houses. They were built of uncut stones, rounded boulders put together with what must have been great labour. The vanished people, lacking other means, moved big rocks mainly by muscle —archaeologists conclude that the Mookini Heiau on Hawaii, one of the largest temples in all of the islands, was built by 15,000 men standing three feet apart, who passed stones a distance of nine miles from their source to the building site. Most of the house platforms in the canyon were scarcely recognizable, their stones shoved apart and scattered by trees growing up among them. Still it appeared that there had once been a fair-sized settlement there. The remains of a five-terraced *heiau*, 180 feet high, stand against the cliff.

The trail, passing close to the old platforms, probably followed the path used by the Hawaiians centuries ago. There was nowhere else to put one. The trees of course were different but the contour of the land, offering not much choice as to where a man could walk, very likely had changed only a little. There were so few level campsites that when we came to a flat place 20 feet wide under a big *kukui* tree I suggested to Herbst that we return there at the end of the day.

He glanced at the Hawaiian stonework near by and grinned. "You're not afraid of *akua*?"

Akua are spirits or ghosts. They wander everywhere in the islands and are thought to be fond of haunting the ruins of old houses and *heiau*. I said I had always wanted to see a ghost and had gone out of my way to hunt for them but had had bad luck. Wherever I had looked for ghosts, in attics and cemeteries, haunted houses and canyons, they had never allowed me to see them. Ghosts had no faith in me.

We went on walking. The thought of Herbst's tree was always somewhere in my mind. If he said that we would have to climb 800 feet straight up the canyon wall to reach the tree I would have started looking for ways to do it.

It struck me that we had been making our way along the trail for at least an hour but the hands of my watch had not moved much. They seemed frozen at 10 minutes past three.

"What time is it?"

"About five after four."

The watch was running but the second hand was barely moving, creeping along at one-third speed or even less. It appeared that it was taking three or four minutes to go once around the dial. It was the best watch I had ever had, a gold electric watch powered by a little battery the size of a dime. It had always been remarkably accurate, within one or two seconds a day. I had owned it for four years. Only 30 days ago it had been cleaned and a new battery had been put in. Batteries are good for about a year. I set the watch at five minutes past four to match Herbst's and we moved on.

He walked ahead of me on the narrow trail. The tree would be on the right-hand side, he said. He hoped I would not be disappointed in it. It had finished flowering by now, and in any case the flowers were not very dramatic. He spoke like a man who is very proud of a beautiful daughter but feels obliged for modesty's sake to point out that she has a couple of freckles.

We went on for another half mile. Herbst slowed his pace, seeming to be puzzled, and at length he said, "I think somehow we may have walked *past* it. Let's go a little way more to make sure, and then turn around." Soon we reached a place where we could descend to the stream. After we had rested for a few minutes on the rocks, drinking the sweet water, he said, "Yes, we're past it. I don't know how I could have missed it, but I did".

We turned and began to go back over the trail. There was no use in my trying to look for the tree because I would not have recognized it, but Herbst gave me a description of its setting—the slope, the rocks, the way the ground fell off steeply on the right, a fallen sisal pole—and I looked for that combination.

After a few minutes he glanced at me over his shoulder, grinning again. "Do you think it's one of those things that appear only once every hundred years?"

It was profoundly quiet in that place. No birds sang and no breeze stirred in the trees. Once we heard the bleat of a goat somewhere on the cliffs overhead but there was no other sound except that of our own footsteps.

"It can't be far," he said. "This part of the trail is very familiar."

I stopped to retie the lace on one of my boots and Herbst walked on ahead, around a corner and out of sight. In a minute he reappeared, his fist raised. "Found it!"

The *Hibiscadelphus* trees were on a very steep, shady slope among boulders and ledges. *Wiliwili* and *kukui* overtopped them, cutting off much of the direct sunlight. Herbst pointed to a particular *Hibiscadelphus* and said, "That's the type tree, the one we'll describe".

In establishing a new species botanists select for description a representative individual, a "type specimen", having the characteristics by which others of its kind may be recognized. As we pulled ourselves up the slope towards it Herbst pointed out the five others near by, all of them within a radius of 50 feet, standing among taller trees. Two were immature and three, reaching up through the shadows towards the light, had thin, leggy trunks. The type tree was more compact and better shaped. It was about 20 feet tall, like the other members of the genus de-

A new species of Hibiscadelphus tree whose existence was not even suspected before 1972 was discovered in a small canyon on the island of Kauai by Dr. Derral Herbst of the Pacific Tropical Botanical Garden. Until Herbst's find, botanists believed that all species of the Hibiscadelphus genus were highly specialized and existed almost exclusively on the island of Hawaii. The Kauai discovery suggests that Hibiscadelphus is the frail relic of a genus once widespread and thriving throughout the islands.

NEWLY DISCOVERED HIBISCADELPHUS (FOREGROUND)

FULLY OPENED BLOOM

LICHEN-COVERED BARK

SPENT BLOOM AND BRACTS

scribed long ago by Joseph Rock, with a trunk perhaps five inches in diameter at the base. There was a main crotch only a couple of feet up from the ground, and above that the tree branched and rebranched as gracefully as a small elm. The bark was smooth and dark grey, the leaves roughly heart shaped, three or four inches long with toothed edges. They were widely spaced on the branches, like ornaments, five or six inches apart. I found myself counting them and when I had ticked off a few dozen on one large branch I estimated that there were only about 600 leaves on the entire tree. The flowers had all disappeared. Later Herbst showed me one that he had collected on his first visit and placed in a bottle of preserving fluid: tubular, curved, yellow-green on the outside and yellowish within. Later still, weeks after I had returned to the mainland, Herbst sent me the opening sentences of the Latin description. "Remember," he wrote, "botanical Latin is a breed unto itself." The description began: *Arbores sex coronis rotundatis cinerascentibus usque 5 m. altas truncis 5-8 cm. diametro novimus. Ramuli novelli internodiis 0.5-10 cm. longis tomentulo pilorum stellatorum vestiuntur.* Beneath this he affixed a translation: "We know six trees with rounded greyish crowns up to 5 metres high and trunks 5-8 cm. in diameter. The young branches, with internodes 0.5-10 cm. long are clothed with a felt of star-shaped hairs."

I sat on a rock and stared at the tree while he climbed up and down the slope searching for others. He seemed not to expect to find any more, and did not. When he returned I asked him how old he thought the type tree might be.

"Impossible to tell, really. If I had to guess I'd say it was twenty-five or thirty. It doesn't look like much, does it? I mean, nurseries all over the world aren't going to start propagating it like mad."

I felt as though someone had spoken ill of *my* daughter and started to say, "Now, dammit, it's . . ." when I realized that it was scarcely necessary to take the tree's part in talking to Herbst, of all people.

We climbed down to the trail. The second hand on my watch was still almost invisibly dragging itself along. The watch now said 10 after four and according to Herbst's the time was quarter past six. "Do you suppose ghosts don't like gadgets like this?" I asked. If I were an old Hawaiian *akua*, and someone came into my canyon wearing a gold electric watch, I would treat him badly. A man like that might be capable of putting up a big plastic hotel.

"Possibly they don't like mechanical things in general," Herbst said. "Twice in the last year when I've been driving through Knudsen Gap in the middle of the night alone, my car has stopped running and I've had to walk. Knudsen Gap is supposed to be a good place for *akua*."

"How did it stop? No gas? No ignition?"

"It just stopped. When I went back next day it ran all right."

Herbst does not believe in ghosts any more than I do. We dropped the subject. I wanted to explore one part of the canyon and he had it in mind to look at another. We separated, agreeing to meet in about an hour at the place where we had stopped to drink from the stream.

Dusk comes early and fast in the bottoms of narrow canyons. From down there the stars are visible sooner than they are from the rims. It was the unexpected glimpse of a star that made me realize how far the day had ebbed. There was still some light left when I reached the place where we were to meet, but Herbst was not there. I sat down to wait for him. There was nothing to do except cut the corner off a plastic bag of dehydrated beef stew, pour in water from the stream and let it soak. I doubted that the *akua* would admire that very much, either.

Herbst seemed to be taking a prodigious time to get there. Soon it would be too dark to move around. In fact it was already almost too dark. Then I remembered that we had drunk from the stream not once but twice. Now I was deep in the canyon and he was waiting for me down near its mouth where we had first stopped. We should have had a better understanding.

It seemed worth an effort to try to reach him but after only a few minutes of hurrying along the narrow trail I had to slow down. As the darkness deepened I looked for a flat spot to lie down for the night. Soon I came to the *Hibiscadelphus* trees, or at any rate to a place on the trail not far from them, and found a level patch of ground about six feet by three between the trail and a big rock. Home.

The night was not yet full black. In the shadows I could see, very dimly, the type tree on the slope above me. I ate the cold beef stew and stretched out flat. I was not directly in the trail but only about a foot away from it. Goats and wild pigs used the trail and for a moment I wondered about them. Goats are timid and no problem, but I was not sure about pigs. I had heard that big boars will sometimes go after a man and I did not care much for the notion of tangling with a 250-pound pig in the dark; but there was not much to be done about that except squeeze up against the rock and get as far off the trail as I could, so the pig would have plenty of room to get by.

I awakened three or four times during the night and looked by habit at the luminous dial of the watch. I could not believe what the hands said but the watch was still running—it makes a faint humming sound like the dial tone in a telephone. Aside from that ridiculous noise, which can be heard only at a distance of an inch or two, there was not one sound in the canyon. Each time I awakened I became increasingly conscious of the *Hibiscadelphus* tree on the slope above me. So powerful an aura of life was emanating from the tree that I could feel it. Somehow the tree was establishing itself as an individual presence up there in the dark. I could sense its life, as a blind man is said to sense upon entering a silent room that someone else is there.

When I think about it today I try to convince myself that the case was really the other way round: I was only attributing the supernatural presence to the tree because I felt strongly about it, the best of only six on this planet. After incalculable years of evolution, millions of unknown sunsets and sunrises, the species had at last come to the end of its line. There is something deeply sad and touching about the last living thing of its kind standing with its back against the wall. But of course the species will not die now—Herbst has seeds from the tree, they have germinated, and he is watching the young plants closely.

Before dawn two jungle fowl, a long way off towards the head of the canyon, began to crow. They were brought to the islands by Polynesians long ago, escaped, and reverted to their original wild state. Jungle fowl have regained the power of vigorous flight although, like pheasants, they rarely fly long distances. The cocks are small and quite beautiful. Their hackles may be gold, bodies steel grey with russet bands, tails long, arched and black and white. The two cocks crowed alternately and the sky turned from grey to rose.

The canyon was filled with morning mist. I climbed the slope to the tree, putting my hand on it to keep from sliding back. A magical air of life like the mist flickered round it. Touching the bark, I imagined a thousand tiny pulses within the tree. I could sense its roots in the earth, curling around buried stones, weaving in the ashes of long-quenched cooking fires, drawing up moisture that passed through the trunk to the topmost leaves and vanished in the brightening air.

With all my heart I wished the tree well. I even looked to see if there was anything I might possibly do to help it. But there were no strangling vines or parasitic plants growing on it that I could remove, or any rocks farther up the slope poised to slide down on it, that perhaps I could shove aside. I took a leaf from the tree and put it carefully in my pocket, went down the slope, put on my pack and set out to find Herbst.

Nothing had been walking along the trail during the night. I broke a good many fresh spiderwebs as I passed, and noticed some that were so low to the ground that a pig would have broken them too. Several giant toads, larger than a man's fist, had taken up positions of ambush on the trail and beside it, waiting for breakfast to come wandering past. The toads are not native to the islands but to Mexico and South America. They were imported to deal primarily with sugar beetles and the very plentiful cockroaches. Occasionally they also eat Hawaiian centipedes, imported too, which attain lengths of seven or eight inches and can give a man a bite he will remember for 13 years.

Herbst was waiting for me some miles away beside the trail. He knew that I would have to pass him on my way out. No, he hadn't given much thought to our failure to meet on the preceding evening. In fact, he said cheerfully, he supposed the failure had been deliberate on my part. Since I seemed to like the wilderness so much he thought I had probably wanted to be alone in it.

It was 8:30 by Herbst's watch. Mine was about five hours behind. But the second hand seemed to be moving briskly again so I set the watch and we began to climb out of Waimea Canyon. It is not really an arduous climb but it does discourage conversation. In two and a half miles the trail ascends nearly twice the height of the Empire State Building. Beneath the weight of his pack a man feels very physical, indrawn, his mind turning over slowly. He does not solve many problems except where to put his feet.

We stopped to rest fairly often, and after a couple of hours I compared our watches. Mine was running normally again. It is still running normally to this day, with the same battery, and has not faltered once. It seemed to me that a speck of dirt must have gotten into the mechanism, impeded it for several hours, and then worked itself loose. As I plodded up the trail I was sure that much the same thing had happened to Herbst's car when it had mysteriously stopped during the night.

Near the end of the climb I turned to look down in the direction of the tree. I could not even see the mouth of the side canyon where it was growing but I could feel its presence down there. Today, 5,000 miles away, I feel it still.

Isolation on a Far Shore

PHOTOGRAPHS BY DAN BUDNIK

For some visitors, the Na Pali coast on the uninhabited northwest face of the island of Kauai evokes a sense of timelessness. Photographer Dan Budnik, who studied Na Pali's rugged profile from the air, from the sea and on the ground, came away with an impression of time in its most rudimentary meaning. Being at Na Pali, he reports, was "like being at the beginning of the world—or the end".

A walk along an 11-mile strip of this sea- and rain-washed shore afforded Budnik a microcosmic view of the entire Hawaiian archipelago. The coast takes its name from the Hawaiian word *pali*, meaning steep cliffs, like those that make up a good part of the coast (*opposite*). Some of them, composed of lava from volcanoes long extinct, drop from heights of 3,000 feet to the ocean and penetrate deep below its surface; here and there they are pierced with tunnels that once channelled molten lava, or are overhung with arches carved by the pounding surf, like the site shown on pages 178-179. The cliffs vary in colour from gleaming blue-black to dull russet, depending on the mineral composition of the lava and on changing reflections of the sun's rays from sky and sea.

In some places the path along the coast opens on beaches of inviting white coral sand carried in by the surf from eroding coral reefs offshore. At other places, the way skirts beds of football-sized rocks (*page 177*). Still other stretches of the shore adjoin slopes of lava, so softened and broken by weathering that it can crumble to cinders underfoot, and must be avoided.

Where the path turns inland it follows a number of valleys—some as hemmed in as grottoes, others wide and spacious as amphitheatres. The earth is lush with exotic bird's-nest fern, thin-trunked, scarlet-flowering *ohia lehua* trees and sandalwood trees with purple blossoms. Waterfalls flash rainbows and carve gullies in the mountainsides.

Not even traces of a past civilization could diminish Budnik's feeling of wilderness isolation. When in the interior he came on stone walls built by Polynesian settlers some 1,200 years ago, he was struck by their failure to conjure up a picture of human habitation. "How different from Robert Frost's notion that 'good fences make good neighbours'," Budnik says. "These walls, far from closing you in, seem, like the very vegetation among which they stand, to grow right out of the earth."

PLUNGING SEA CLIFFS AT KAILIU POINT

A TIDAL POOL ON KALALAU BEACH

KUKUI TREES IN THE NUALOLO VALLEY

OHIA LEHUA TREES CLINGING TO A VALLEY SLOPE

THE NA PALI COASTLINE FROM KEE BEACH TO KALALAU

MAIDENHAIR FERNS AND BRACKET FUNGUS IN HANAKAPIAI VALLEY

BIRD'S-NEST FERN NEAR THE RIVER HANAKAPIAI

A VALLEY WATERFALL, INLAND FROM HANAKAPIAI BEACH

RED HILL, RUSTY WITH IRON OXIDES, ABOVE KALALAU BEACH

SURF-ROUNDED LAVA COBBLES ON KALALAU BEACH

WAVE-CUT OVERHANG AND CORAL SAND AT KALALAU BEACH

Bibliography

†*Available only in paperback.*

Day, A. Grove, *Hawaii and Its People.* Meredith, 1968.

Emerson, Nathaniel B., *Unwritten Literature of Hawaii.* Charles Tuttle, 1965.

†Gosline, William A., and Vernon E. Brock, *Handbook of Hawaiian Fishes.* University of Hawaii Press, 1960.

Handy, E. S. Craighill and Elizabeth Green, *Native Planters in Old Hawaii.* Bishop Museum Press, 1972.

Herbert, Don and Bardossi Fulvio, *Kilauea: Case History of a Volcano.* Harper and Row, 1968.

King, Judith E., *Seals of the World.* British Museum, (Nat. History), 1964.

Kuck, Loraine E., and Richard C. Tongg, *Hawaiian Flowers and Flowering Trees.* Tuttle, Tokyo.

Macdonald, Gordon A., and Agatin T. Abbott, *Volcanoes in the Sea.* University of Hawaii Press, 1970.

Maxwell, Gavin, *Seals of the World.* World of Wildlife Series, Constable, 1967.

Munro, George C., *Birds of Hawaii.* Charles Tuttle.

Stearns, Harold T., *Geology of the State of Hawaii.* Pacific Books, 1966.

Tomich, P. Quentin, *Mammals in Hawaii.* Bishop Museum Press, 1969.

Wenkam, Robert, *Maui.* Friends of the Earth, 1970.

Westervelt, William D., *Hawaiian Legends of Volcanoes.* Charles Tuttle.

†Zimmerman, Elwood C., *Insects of Hawaii.* University of Hawaii Press. 1948.

Acknowledgments

The author and editors of this book are particularly indebted to Robert Wenkam, Honolulu, Hawaii, and Richard E. Warner, Foundation of Environmental Biology, Berkeley, California. They also wish to thank the following: Winston Banko, U.S. Bureau of Sport Fisheries and Wildlife, Hawaii National Park, Hawaii; Robert Bone, Honolulu, Hawaii; Sherwin Carlquist, Horton Professor of Botany, Claremont Graduate School, Claremont, California; F. Raymond Fosberg, special adviser in tropical biology, Smithsonian Institution, Washington, D.C.; Bryan Harry, Superintendent, Hawaii National Park, Hawaii; Derral Herbst, Botanist, Pacific Tropical Botanical Garden, Hawaii; Sidney S. Horenstein, Department of Invertebrate Paleontology, The American Museum of Natural History, New York City; James E. Kaina, Hawaii Visitors Bureau, New York City; Tom Kaser, Honolulu, Hawaii; John I. Kjargaard, Department of Entomology, University of Hawaii, Honolulu; Eugene Kridler, U.S. Bureau of Sport Fisheries and Wildlife, Hawaii; A. Jackson Lynn Jr., The Nature Conservancy, Arlington, Virginia; Larry G. Pardue, The New York Botanical Garden, New York City; Donald W. Peterson, scientist in charge, and the staff of Hawaiian Volcano Observatory, Hawaii; Don Reeser, Park Biologist, Hawaii National Park, Hawaii; John L. Sincock, U.S. Bureau of Sport Fisheries and Wildlife, Hawaii.

Picture Credits

Sources for pictures in this book are shown below. Credits for pictures from left to right are separated by commas, from top to bottom by dashes.

Cover—Fred Stimson. Front end papers 2, 3—David Muench. Front end paper 4, page 1—Dick Schmidt. 2, 3 —Dan Budnik. 4 to 9—David Cavagnaro. 10, 11—Robert Wenkam. 12, 13—Dan Budnik. 18, 19—Maps by R. R. Donnelley Cartographic Services. 24, 25—Robert Wenkam. 28—The New York Public Library. 30, 31—Aaron Dygart. 35—Richard Warner. 36, 37 —Donald W. Peterson. 38, 39—David Mowat, Hawaiian Volcano Observatory, U.S. Geological Survey photo by Gordon A. MacDonald. 40, 41—Robert Wenkam. 42, 43—David Muench, Robert Wenkam. 44, 45—Dan Budnik, Robert Wenkam. 46, 47—Rick Grigg, David Cavagnaro. 54, 55—Georg Gerster from Rapho Guillumette. 58, 59 —David Cavagnaro. 64, 65—Hawaiian Volcano Observatory, W. E. Ferguson—David Cavagnaro. 68 to 79 —David Cavagnaro. 85—Robert Wenkam. 87—Richard Warner. 90, 91 —Robert Wenkam. 95—Robert Wenkam. 99 to 105—Dan Budnik. 108—Map by R. R. Donnelley Cartographic Services. 110, 111—David Cavagnaro. 115—David Cavagnaro. 121 to 135—David Cavagnaro. 140, 141—Dan Budnik. 144—Culver Pictures. 146—Dan Budnik. 152—David Cavagnaro. 155—John Zoiner. 159 —Rick Golt. 165 to 179—Dan Budnik.

Index

*Numerals in italics indicate a
photograph or drawing of the subject
mentioned.*

Filmsetting by C. E. Dawkins (Typesetters) Ltd., London, SE1 1UN.
Printed and bound in Belgium by Brepols S.A.—Turnhout.